Thriving Without Fear in the Age of Artificial Intelligence (AI)

Dr. Sylvester Cotton

Praise for Thriving Without Fear

"This book gave me the confidence I needed to attempt using AI, and it was written in layman's terms. Thanks, Dr. Cotton." — **J.W. Carson, CPA, Horn Lake, MS**

"I started using AI immediately in my medical practice after reading the book. I followed the book example, and I felt as if I had a personal assistant instantly." — **G. W. Campbell, MD, Columbia, SC**

"The book gave me the desperate push that I needed to understand AI and to start using it daily." — **E. Benson, CISO, St Louis, MO**

"After reading the book, I felt as if I was ready to use AI in every aspect of my daily life." — **C. Anderson, Business Owner, Tyler, TX**

"The content is such an imperative for those who are reluctant to use AI" — **J.B. Wilson, Hotel Manager, Atlanta, GA**

Dedication:

To everyone who has ever looked at a new piece of technology and wondered if the world was moving too fast without them, this book is for you. Your courage to stay curious, your willingness to try again, and your belief that growth is still possible at every age are the heartbeat of these pages. May you always recognize the strength you already carry and the wisdom that can't be replaced by any machine.

And to the families, caregivers, teachers, builders, and everyday heroes who continue to show up with patience, humor, and hope, thank you. You remind us that the most powerful force in any era isn't the technology we create, but the humanity we bring to it. May this book be a companion on your journey, a steady voice reminding you that the future is not something to fear, but something you are more than ready to shape.

About the Author:

Dr. Sylvester "Sly" Cotton is a seasoned cybersecurity/Artificial Intelligence leader whose career spans more than three decades across the U.S. Army, the Department of Defense, and the defense industry. Known for advancing cyber operations, data analytics, AI integration, and elite cyber training, he played a central role in shaping modern military cyber capabilities. His service includes key command and staff positions, combat leadership as the Multi-National Division CIO/G6 during Operation Iraqi Freedom 06–08, and guiding the historic transition of the Signal Center of Excellence into the Cyber Center of Excellence at Fort Gordon. His strategic vision also drove the integration of Electronic Warfare into cyberspace operations, reinforcing his reputation as a pioneer of convergent warfare.

Beyond government service, Dr. Cotton's impact extends into academia and industry, with influential roles at Unisys, Engility/SAIC, CALIBRE Systems, and Jacobs. His academic foundation-a doctorate in Information Systems and Technology Management, two master's degrees, and a business degree-reflects a blend of technical depth and strategic insight. Coupled with professional credentials such as PMP and ITIL Service Manager, he is widely recognized for elevating standards across cyber operations and technology-driven programs. Dr. Cotton's career illustrates a rare combination of innovation, leadership, and long-term commitment to strengthening the nation's digital resilience.

An AI Survival Guide

Contents

Chapter 1: Why AI Feels Scary (and Why You Can't Afford to Ignore It)

The First Reaction, "This Is Too Much"

When I first introduced a friend of mine, Carol, to AI, she froze. Carol is sharp, resourceful, and the kind of person who has managed life's twists with steady hands. But the moment she opened a simple AI tool on her laptop; her fingers hovered over the keyboard like she was about to set off an alarm. "I don't even know what button to push," she whispered. There was no button, really, just a blinking cursor waiting for her to type. That little blinking line felt intimidating, as though it were silently saying, prove you belong here. Carol laughed nervously, but beneath her laugh was a very real discomfort. "This isn't for me," she said. "It's for the kids. They grew up with this."

Her reaction isn't unusual. In fact, it's one of the most common responses I've seen when people encounter AI for the first time. There's a wave of hesitation, followed by the fear of looking foolish, and then a quiet thought: Maybe it's too late for me to learn this. If you've ever felt that way, you're not alone. AI has been hyped as the "future of everything." We're told it's reshaping industries, changing how we live, even rewriting what it means to be human.

That kind of language can overwhelm anyone. Add in news stories about robots taking jobs, machines "thinking" for themselves, or deepfakes fooling millions, and the whole subject starts to feel less like progress and more like a threat. It's no wonder people freeze up. But here's the truth: AI feels scary not because it's impossible to learn, but because it's unfamiliar. And unfamiliarity has always been intimidating.

Do you remember the first time you used an ATM? The first time you tried to send an email? The first time you saw a smartphone and thought, why would anyone want to carry the internet in their pocket? Fear shows up at the beginning of every new chapter. But in every one of those cases, once you stepped in, the fear shrank. AI is the same.

The Three Big Fears

Whenever I talk to people about AI, three fears almost always appear.

1. **"I'll be replaced."**

   The first and biggest fear is this: If AI can write, speak, analyze, and create, what's left for me? This is not a silly question. It's serious because for decades, we've been warned about "robots replacing workers." And the headlines today often make it sound like the machines are finally here to do just that. Yes, AI can automate certain tasks and routine, repetitive work, like filling out forms, sorting data, or generating the first draft of a document. Some jobs will certainly change, and some tasks will be automated.

   But here's what's missing from the fear: AI does not have judgment, context, or wisdom. It can write a letter, but it cannot decide whether sending that letter is the right thing to do. It can summarize medical research, but it cannot weigh your family history, your personal values, or your intuition. It can generate artwork, but it cannot feel joy, sorrow, or purpose in the act of creating. AI replaces tasks, not people.

Think of it this way: if your job, or your life, was only a stack of repetitive tasks, maybe you'd worry. But if your value comes from experience, relationships, creativity, or leadership, you're not replaceable. In fact, your value increases because AI clears space for those very human qualities. The world doesn't need fewer humans. It needs humans who are freed up to do the parts of life and work that only humans can do.

2. "I can't learn this."

The second fear comes from a place of self-doubt. This is too technical. I'll never figure it out. It's for the next generation, not me. I've heard this countless times. And yet, every time, it turns out to be wrong. Most AI tools today are built to be used in plain language. You don't need to know code. You don't need a manual. You don't even need to understand how it works under the hood. You literally type a question or request, just like you'd text a friend, and the AI responds. That's it.

One man I know, Dave, admitted he was terrified to try. His granddaughter encouraged him: "Just ask it the way you'd ask me."

He typed, give me three dinner ideas using chicken and broccoli. Within seconds, he had a weeknight menu with recipes.
Dave leaned back and said, "That's it? I thought I needed to speak in computer language."

The hardest part isn't the tool; it's the belief that you can't learn. But the truth is, you've learned new skills all your life. You learned to drive. You learned to use a bank machine. You learned how to navigate smartphones, online shopping, and maybe even video calls with your family. AI isn't harder. It just looks different at first.

3. "It's too late for me."

This is the fear that hits deepest. It's the quiet voice that says: I missed the boat.
AI is for younger people. My time has passed. But think about your own journey. When did you first use email? For many, not until adulthood. When did you first search online or use GPS? For many, well into middle age.

You adapted to every one of those shifts, and you found ways to make them work for you. It's never too late because AI doesn't reward who started first, it rewards who starts at all. I once spoke to a retired nurse who believed she was "too old" to try. Her daughter showed her how to use AI to organize her medical notes into a family health log. The nurse said, "I thought I was behind, but now I see I can still use what I know. AI just makes it easier." You haven't missed the boat. You're standing at the dock, and the boat is still loading passengers.

Why Fear Is Natural

Let's pause here. Before we go any further, I want you to know something important: feeling afraid of AI doesn't mean you're weak, outdated, or behind. It means you're human. Fear is how we're wired. Our ancestors survived by being cautious. They hesitated before eating a strange fruit or approaching a new animal. That hesitation protected them. Today, that same wiring makes us hesitate before stepping into new technology. It whispers: Be careful.

You don't know what this is yet. That's not failure, it's self-preservation. But fear isn't the end of the story. Fear is the beginning. Fear means you're awake, paying attention. And once you look closer, fear can transform into focus. Think about the first time you drove on the highway. Your heart may have raced, your grip tight on the wheel. But after some practice, the fear faded, replaced by confidence. AI works the same way. The fear you feel now is simply the tension of standing at the edge of something new. Once you take the first steps, that tension eases. Fear doesn't mean stop. It means pay attention, and then step forward.

Truth vs. Hype

One of the biggest reasons people feel uneasy about AI is the way it's talked about. The headlines scream: "AI will steal your job!" or "Robots are taking over!" Hollywood gives us movies where machines become self-aware and decide humans are expendable. It makes for great entertainment, but it isn't reality.

Let's strip away the noise and separate truth from hype.

- Hype: AI will become conscious.

Truth: AI doesn't "think." It recognizes patterns in data. It doesn't have feelings, desires, or opinions. It's not plotting against anyone. It's simply very fast at connecting dots.

Think of AI like a calculator on steroids. A calculator doesn't know math; it just processes numbers based on formulas. Similarly, AI doesn't know things; it predicts patterns based on the information it's been given.

- Hype: AI will destroy millions of jobs.

Truth: AI will certainly change jobs. But every major technology shift has created new kinds of work even as it made old tasks obsolete. Remember when ATMs arrived? The fear was that bank tellers would disappear. In reality, ATMs took over routine transactions, but banks actually hired more tellers for customer service and relationship roles. The job didn't vanish; it shifted. The same thing is happening with AI. Certain tasks may be automated, but new opportunities are opening for people who know how to guide, check, and apply AI results.

- Hype: AI is too complicated for everyday people.

Truth: AI has never been more approachable. You don't need special training. You don't need to "speak computer." You literally type what you want in plain language, and it responds. It's like having an eager assistant who doesn't mind you being specific or vague, formal or casual.

Try it once, and you'll see it's less about complexity and more about curiosity.

Why Starting Now Matters

Some people say, "I'll wait until the dust settles. Let the younger folks figure it out first." That might sound sensible, but here's the problem: by waiting, you make the climb steeper later. Think of learning AI like learning to swim. Person A dips their toes in the shallow end. They splash around, practice, and get comfortable. By the time they're ready for deeper water, they've built confidence.

Person B avoids the pool. They say, "Not today. I'll try another time." But the longer they wait, the more intimidating the water looks. When they finally decide to try, the pool is crowded, the waves are bigger, and they feel left behind.

The earlier you start, even with tiny steps, the gentler the slope.

- **Benefit 1: Practice without pressure**

  If you begin now, you can experiment in low-stakes ways. Ask AI to plan a grocery list. Ask it for a three-day road trip itinerary. Ask it to summarize a news article. These aren't life-or-death uses; they're playful experiments.

  Over time, these experiments build confidence, so when you do need AI for something important, you won't be starting from scratch.

- **Benefit 2: Compounding benefits**

The sooner you use AI; the more years you'll have to benefit from it. If AI saves you one hour a week, that's 52 hours a year, more than two full days. Multiply that over a decade, and you've saved months of your life. Imagine what you could do with that time: travel, learn, rest, and connect with family.

- **Benefit 3: Your voice matters**

Here's something people rarely consider: the future of AI will be shaped by the people who use it. If only younger generations adopt it, then their needs, their habits, and their perspectives will dominate. But your perspective, your values, your sense of balance, your hard-earned wisdom, is just as important. By using AI, even in small ways, you help shape how it grows. Your voice keeps the future inclusive. Waiting means leaving those decisions to others. Starting now means you get a say.

Guided Exercise, Turning Fear into Opportunity

Now let's make this practical. You don't just need to read about overcoming fear; you need to experience it. Take a blank sheet of paper and draw two columns. On the left, write "Fear." On the right, write "Opportunity." Here's what you'll do: list your three biggest fears about AI in the left column. Then, for each one, write at least one possible opportunity in the right column.

Here are a few examples:

Fear: "AI will take my job." Opportunity: "AI could handle the boring parts so I can focus on meaningful work."

Fear: "AI will confuse me." Opportunity: "AI could explain things in plain language when I don't understand."
Fear: "AI will isolate me." Opportunity: "AI could help me stay connected, reminding me of birthdays, drafting letters, even translating conversations with friends abroad."

Take your time. Write honestly. Don't worry if your opportunities feel small at first.
What matters is flipping the script, moving from fear to possibility. If you want to go deeper, share your list with a trusted friend or family member. Ask them to add one opportunity you might not have thought of. Sometimes others can see potential where we only see risk.

This exercise does two things:

1. It names your fear out loud, which makes it less powerful.
2. It forces your mind to imagine a different outcome, one where AI works for you, not against you. By the time you finish, you'll see that every fear has at least one doorway to opportunity.

A Quick Story, From Fear to Curiosity

I once spoke with a man named Henry. He admitted he was terrified of AI. "It's too much," he said. "I'm too set in my ways." When I asked him to try the Fear-to-Opportunity exercise, his first fear was, "AI will make me feel useless." He stared at the page for a long time before finally writing the opportunity: "Maybe AI could give me new ways to share my experience." The next week, he tried an AI tool to draft a guide for young carpenters, based on his 40 years of experience. The draft wasn't perfect, but it gave him a starting point. He polished it, added stories, and printed copies for his local trade school. Henry went from fearing he'd be replaced to realizing he had more to offer than ever, because AI gave him the leverage to do it faster. That's the power of reframing fear.

Stories of Transformation

The best way to see what's possible is to hear the stories of people who once felt afraid but stepped forward anyway.

- **James, the Retired Teacher**

  James taught history for thirty-five years. After retiring, he thought his teaching days were over. When his daughter mentioned that local students needed tutoring, James hesitated. "I don't know the technology," he said. "Kids today are too advanced." But his grandson showed him how to use AI to draft lesson outlines. The AI produced a rough structure, dates, themes, and key events, which James then enriched with stories, insights, and context. "It gave me the bones," James explained. "I added the heart." Soon, James was tutoring students twice a week. He felt useful again, engaged again, and, this surprised him most, relevant again. AI didn't erase his knowledge; it amplified it.

- **Maria, the Small Business Owner**

  Maria ran a local flower shop. Marketing was her weakness. She dreaded writing social media posts or creating flyers, often avoiding them altogether. "I'm a florist, not a writer," she would say. A friend suggested she try an AI writing tool. Skeptical, Maria typed: Write a cheerful post about spring flowers for my shop, Bloom & Vine. Within seconds, she had three variations. She tweaked the wording, added her personal touch, and posted one. The responses came quickly: new customers, compliments, and even an order for a wedding bouquet.

Maria said, "It felt like having a junior assistant who never complains and works for free." Her business grew 20% that year.

- **Ellen, the Caregiver**

Ellen was caring for her aging mother. Between doctor's appointments, medication schedules, and household tasks, she felt overwhelmed. When she heard about AI reminders and scheduling apps, she resisted. "That's for young people," she muttered. But one evening, after missing a refill date, she decided to try. She asked an AI tool to build a weekly medication reminder schedule. It not only created a calendar but also suggested ways to organize her mother's meals and appointments. "It didn't replace me," Ellen said with relief. "It supported me." The stress lifted. Ellen could focus more on time with her mom and less on juggling details.

These stories are proof: AI doesn't demand expertise. It doesn't require perfection. It just requires willingness. Each of these people started with hesitation. Each found that fear wasn't the end, it was the beginning.

Reflection: Where Am I Resisting Change?

Now it's your turn. Pause for a moment. Think about your life right now. Where are you resisting change? Where do you feel that stubborn pull of "not for me"?

Maybe it's in your work. Maybe it's in your hobbies. Maybe it's in how you manage your household.

Write down your answers to these questions:

1. Where am I holding back from change?
2. What's it costing me, in time, in energy, in peace of mind?
3. If I let AI take on even one small task, what might it free me to do instead?

   Take your time. Write honestly. This is not a test. No one else will see your answers unless you choose to share them. What you're doing here is drawing a map. You're identifying where resistance is strongest so you can decide where curiosity should step in next.

The Surprise of Small Steps

One thing you'll notice when you reflect on resistance: often, the smallest steps lead to the biggest shifts. You don't need to overhaul your life with AI. You don't need to master dozens of tools. You just need one experiment.

- Ask AI to generate a shopping list.
- Ask it to summarize an article you don't have time to read.
- Ask it to draft a letter you've been putting off.

That's it. Small steps. Each step chips away at fear. Each step builds confidence. Each step proves: I can do this. The surprise isn't how powerful AI is. The surprise is how quickly you realize it's manageable.

Closing Summary, Fear as a Doorway

Let's return to Carol, my friend who froze at the blinking cursor.

The first time she saw AI, she felt paralyzed. But a few weeks later, she tried again.

This time, she asked the AI to help her plan a family reunion. It suggested menus, schedules, and even games for the kids. Carol laughed as she scrolled through the suggestions. "I never would have thought of this," she said. She didn't become an expert overnight. She didn't suddenly love technology. But she discovered that AI wasn't a wall blocking her future; it was a doorway to new possibilities. And that's the message I want you to carry as you close this chapter: fear isn't the enemy. Avoidance is.

Fear means you're awake. Fear means you care. Fear means you're standing at the edge of something that matters. If you ignore AI, the world will move forward without you. But if you take even one step, if you let curiosity lead the way, you'll discover that fear shrinks, confidence grows, and opportunities multiply. You don't have to be fearless. You just have to be willing. Fear is not the end. Fear is the beginning. And once you step through, you'll see the future is not something to fear at all, it's something you can shape.

Chapter 2: The History Lesson, We've Done This Before

A Familiar Feeling

When the first microwave ovens appeared in the 1970s, many people wouldn't touch them.

They were suspicious of "radiation cooking" and afraid that food prepared inside might somehow be unsafe.

Some people even kept their microwaves in the garage or basement because they didn't want them near the family table.

Fast forward a decade, and microwaves became a normal fixture in almost every kitchen.

What once seemed threatening became convenient, so convenient that today it's hard to imagine daily life without one.

The microwave isn't unique. Every generation has faced a wave of new technology that seemed intimidating, strange, or even dangerous.

And every time, people eventually found a way not only to accept it but to benefit from it.

Artificial intelligence feels enormous right now. But if you look back, you'll realize: we've done this before.

The Pattern of Resistance

History is full of stories where new technology was met with doubt, fear, and even anger.

Here are just a few:

- **The Telephone**

When Alexander Graham Bell first demonstrated the telephone, critics scoffed. "Why would anyone want to talk to someone miles away?"

Newspapers asked. Many people preferred face-to-face conversations or written letters and said the telephone was unnecessary.

Some feared it would erode the community because people would stop visiting each other.

Today, we carry not only telephones but pocket-sized devices that also serve as cameras, maps, encyclopedias, and entertainment centers.

The telephone didn't destroy community; it created new forms of connection.

- **The Automobile**

When cars began replacing horse-drawn carriages, they were called "devil wagons."

Some cities passed laws requiring a person to walk ahead of each car, waving a red flag to warn pedestrians.

People feared accidents, pollution, and moral decline.

Of course, accidents and pollution did become challenges, but cars also transformed how we live, work, and travel.

Entire economies were reshaped around mobility. What was once a curiosity is now essential.

- **The ATM**

When automated teller machines arrived in the 1960s and 70s, bank tellers worried their jobs would vanish.

Customers worried about trusting a machine with their money. "What if it eats my card? What if it gives me the wrong amount?"

Today, ATMs are ordinary. They didn't eliminate bank tellers; they changed their role.

Tellers shifted from handling routine withdrawals to providing customer service, advice, and complex transactions.

- **The Internet**

When the internet first appeared in homes in the 1990s, many dismissed it as a fad.

"Why would I need email when I can just call?"

"Why would I shop online when I can go to a store?"

Others feared identity theft, fraud, or that it would be too complicated to use.

Look around today. We don't just use the internet, we live on it.

Banking, shopping, working, reading, connecting, it all runs through the web.

The fears didn't vanish overnight, but as familiarity grew, so did trust.

A Predictable Cycle

Every major technology follows the same cycle:

1. **Shock and Suspicion** People react with fear. "This will ruin everything!"
2. **Curiosity and Experimentation:** A few brave souls test it out.
3. **Awkward Use** Early experiences are clumsy and limited. Mistakes happen.
4. **Normalization** The technology improves, gets easier, and more people adopt it.
5. **Integration Eventually**, it becomes invisible, just part of life.

Think about the smartphone in your pocket. The first iPhone appeared in 2007. Less than 20 years later, it's so ingrained that we forget what life was like before.

We don't think about "using a smartphone"; we just live our lives, and the smartphone happens to be there.

Artificial intelligence is at stages 2 and 3 right now.

It's new enough to feel awkward and strange, but familiar enough that people are starting to see the benefits.

Within a few years, it will be so integrated that we'll wonder how we lived without it.

Exercise: Your "I'll Never Use It" Story

Take a moment to think about a technology you once resisted but now use without a second thought.

Maybe it was an email. Maybe it was texting. Maybe it was the ATM.

Write down:

1. What was your first reaction? (Fear, doubt, annoyance?)
2. What finally convinced you to try?
3. How do you use it now?

When you write this down, you'll notice something powerful: you already have a history of overcoming resistance.

AI is just the next chapter.

More Moments of Doubt

The microwave, the telephone, the ATM, we've already seen how skepticism turns into acceptance.

But history offers even more examples of how technology once seemed frightening or absurd, only to become later indispensable.

- **The Light Bulb**

When electric light bulbs first appeared in the late 1800s, many people refused to install them in their homes.

They worried about fires, explosions, or strange effects on health. Gas lamps felt safer because people were familiar with them.

But electric light was cleaner, easier, and safer in the long run. Once neighbors began adopting it, others followed.

Within a few decades, the idea of living without electricity became unimaginable.

- **The Personal Computer**

In the 1970s and early 80s, computers were seen as tools for scientists and businesses, not for everyday households.

Critics said, "Why would anyone need a computer at home?" The machines looked complicated, intimidating, and unnecessary.

By the 1990s, computers had become central to work, learning, and entertainment.

Now, we don't call them "personal computers" anymore; we just call them life.

- **Online Shopping**

When online shopping arrived, people scoffed. "Who would buy something without seeing it first? What about fraud? What if the package never comes?"

The idea of typing in your credit card number on a website felt reckless.

Today, online shopping is routine. From groceries to furniture, we click, pay, and receive deliveries with ease.

In fact, many people shop online more often than they go into stores.

The Social Side of Technology

Each of these examples shows something important: new technology doesn't just change what we do, it changes how society is organized.

- **Jobs shift.** Some roles fade, but others emerge. ATMs reduced the number of cash-handling tasks but increased demand for customer service and banking specialists.
- **Culture adapts.** The telephone made long-distance relationships easier. The car reshaped where people lived, leading to the suburbs.
- **Communities evolve.** The internet created global networks, allowing people to connect across continents.

At first, these changes feel threatening. People worry about what will be lost.

But over time, society finds new rhythms, new opportunities, and new norms.

AI will be no different. Some jobs will shift. Some tasks will disappear. But new opportunities, roles we can't even imagine yet, will emerge. Just as past generations couldn't predict YouTube creators or app developers, we can't yet see every possibility AI will create.

A Story of Change: The Bank Teller

Let's revisit the story of ATMs, because it's one of the clearest parallels to AI.

When ATMs spread in the 1970s, headlines warned of mass unemployment for bank tellers. But what actually happened?

Banks opened more branches because ATMs reduced the cost of running them.

Instead of being eliminated, tellers were retrained to focus on customer relationships, loans, and advice.

By the 1990s, there were actually more bank tellers employed than before ATMs.

Their work shifted from repetitive transactions to higher-value services.

The lesson? Technology rarely eliminates people; it changes their role.

AI will likely follow the same pattern. It will take over the routine tasks, but it will elevate the value of human qualities like empathy, creativity, leadership, and judgment.

Why Fear Often Exaggerates

When we look back at history, one thing becomes clear: fear often exaggerates the downside of new technology while underestimating the upside.

People thought electricity would burn down cities. Instead, it lit them safely.

People thought computers were unnecessary. Instead, they became essential.

People thought online shopping would fail. Instead, it reshaped global retail.

Fear paints a picture of loss. Experience shows us a picture of gain.

This doesn't mean every fear is baseless. New technology does bring challenges. Cars cause traffic accidents and pollution.

The internet created misinformation. AI will also bring risks. But just as we created seatbelts, stoplights, and fact-checking, we will create guardrails for AI.

Fear is natural. But it rarely tells the full story.

Exercise: Looking Back, Looking Forward

Let's make this personal.

Think of a time in your life when you resisted a new technology.

Maybe it was texting.

Maybe it was debit cards.

Maybe it was the GPS on your phone.

Write down:

1. What was your first reaction? (Suspicion? Annoyance?)
2. What finally convinced you to try it?
3. How do you use it today?

Now, ask yourself: What lesson does this story hold for how I approach AI?

Here's an example:

Technology: Online banking.

First reaction: "I'll never trust my money to a website."

What convinced me: My employer stopped mailing paper paychecks.

How I use it today: I check balances daily, pay bills in minutes.

Lesson for AI: I don't have to understand every detail for it to be useful; I just need to trust the system step by step.

Write your own story. When you see how you've already adapted before, you'll gain confidence that you can do it again.

The Bridge Between Past and Present

Looking at the history of technology helps us in two ways:

1. It reminds us we've faced this before. Fear is nothing new. We doubted microwaves, light bulbs, cars, and computers.
We adapted every time.

2. It shows us the rhythm of change. First fear, then curiosity, then awkward trial, then normalization, then invisibility.
AI is simply in the "awkward trial" stage.
Once you recognize the pattern, AI stops looking like an alien invasion and starts looking like the next chapter in a very familiar story.

How Society Learns Together

Change is rarely something individuals face alone. More often, we learn in groups.

When home computers first arrived, there were neighborhood clubs where people gathered in church basements or community centers to share tips. They traded floppy disks, taught each other how to load programs, and laughed at their mistakes.

When the internet spread, schools and libraries became teaching hubs.

Adults signed up for evening classes to learn how to send emails or use search engines.

People leaned on their kids and grandkids for help. Families became mini "tech support teams."

We are social learners. That's how we've always adapted.

The same will be true for AI. You don't have to figure it out in isolation.

In fact, you'll learn faster and with less fear if you involve others.

A friend, a family member, a coworker, a local group. The journey becomes lighter when you share it.

The Power of Curiosity

Think back to the telephone, the car, or the computer.

The people who thrived weren't the ones who understood every wire or engine part.

They were the ones who stayed curious.

They asked questions.

They tried small experiments.

They laughed at their mistakes and tried again.

Curiosity beats expertise every time when facing new technology.

AI is no different. You don't need to master the algorithms behind it.

You just need to stay curious enough to ask: What happens if I try this?

That mindset turns fear into discovery.

Lessons for AI From History

So, what can we carry forward from our past experiences into this new AI era?

- **Lesson 1: You've Adapted Before**

  If you've ever used a smartphone, an ATM, or online shopping, you've already proven you can learn.

  AI is simply another tool waiting for you to explore.

- **Lesson 2: Small Steps Work**

Nobody jumped into online banking by wiring thousands of dollars on day one. They started small, checking balances, paying one bill.

Do the same with AI: ask it to draft a shopping list, or write a poem for a birthday card.

Small steps build trust.

- **Lesson 3: Resistance Fades with Use**

The first time you tried GPS, you probably double-checked the directions. Now, you follow the voice without thinking.

The awkwardness disappears with repetition. AI feels strange now, but the more you use it, the more natural it will feel.

- **Lesson 4: Human Qualities Remain Essential**

Every major technology took over repetitive or mechanical tasks, but never replaced human judgment, relationships, or creativity.

AI will be the same. What makes you human becomes even more valuable.

Reflection: Your "Next Step" Story

Take out your notebook. Answer these questions:

1. When I think about AI, what is my strongest hesitation?
2. If I imagine myself five years from now, using AI comfortably, what might that look like?
3. What is one small, safe way I could try AI this week?

Examples might include:

- Asking it to plan a three-day meal schedule.
- Having it explains a confusing medical article in plain language.
- Asking it to draft a thank-you note you've been meaning to send.

The goal isn't to become an expert. The goal is to take one step from hesitation to action.

Story: From Doubt to Delight

Margaret, a grandmother of four, swore she would never "mess with robots." Her granddaughter convinced her to try once.

Margaret typed: Write a bedtime story for a five-year-old about a bear who loves pancakes.

The AI produced a short, whimsical tale. Margaret read it aloud, adding her own flair and silly voices.

Her grandson laughed so hard he begged for another.

The next day, Margaret told me, "I thought AI was cold and mechanical. But that story warmed my heart. It wasn't perfect, but it gave me a starting point. I made it my own."

Her fear melted into delight. And that's the point: AI isn't here to take away your voice, it's here to give you more ways to use it.

Closing Summary: You've Done This Before

Let's step back.

Every generation has faced new technologies that felt overwhelming:

- The telephone that "would ruin conversation."
- The car that was called a "devil wagon."
- The ATM that "would put people out of work."
- The internet that was "too complicated for normal folks."

Each time, we adapted. Each time, society adjusted. Each time, what once felt frightening became ordinary.

Artificial intelligence is simply the next chapter in that story. It feels strange now, but soon it will feel familiar.

The cycle never changes, only the tools do.

The lesson of history is simple: you are more adaptable than you think.

You don't need to be fearless. You just need to be willing. You've done it before.

You can do it again.

Chapter 3: AI in Plain English

The Invisible Assistant

Last year, my neighbor Paul mentioned he had never used AI.

"That stuff is for scientists," he said, waving his hand dismissively.

I smiled and asked him, "Do you ever watch Netflix?" "Of course," he replied. "And do you ever wonder how it knows what shows to recommend?" He paused.

"I guess I never thought about it." "That's AI," I told him.

Paul frowned, then laughed. "Wait, you mean I've been using AI without realizing it?"

Exactly.

AI is already woven into everyday life, often in ways you don't see.

It decides which ads appear on your screen, how your phones autocorrect finishes your text, how your bank detects fraud, and how your maps reroute you around traffic. You may think you're not part of the AI revolution. But the truth is: you already are. What AI Really Is (Without the Jargon)

Let's strip AI down to its simplest definition.

Artificial Intelligence is a set of tools that spot patterns and make predictions based on data. That's it.

It doesn't think. It doesn't dream. It doesn't have feelings or opinions.

It's a calculator that works with words, pictures, sounds, and numbers instead of just digits.

Here's a simple way to think about it:

- A **calculator** answers: *What's 347 times 29?*

- AI answers: What's a polite way to write a thank-you note?

Both are pattern machines. One is math. The other is language, images, or behaviors.

AI works by training on examples. Just as a child learns language by hearing words repeated, AI learns by processing billions of examples of text, pictures, or sound.

Then, when you ask it a question, it predicts what "should" come next based on those patterns.

For example:

You type: Write me a recipe with chicken and broccoli.

The AI has seen thousands of recipes with those ingredients.

It predicts a reasonable recipe format: ingredients, steps, and cooking times.

Out comes a recipe.

There's no magic. Just very fast pattern recognition.

Where AI Already Lives in Your Life

If you think you're not using AI, let's pull back the curtain.

Here are some everyday examples where AI already works quietly in the background:

- **Autocorrect and Text Suggestions**

When you type a message on your phone, and it suggests the next word, that's AI.

It predicts what word usually follows the one you just typed.

- **Online Recommendations**

Netflix, Amazon, Spotify, and YouTube; their recommendations are powered by AI.

They study your past choices and compare them to millions of other people to predict what you might like next.

- **Fraud Detection**

Your bank uses AI to spot unusual transactions. If you normally shop in Atlanta and suddenly there's a charge in Paris, AI flags it instantly.

- **Voice Assistants**

"Hey Siri," "Alexa," "OK Google", these are AI systems trained to recognize speech and respond with useful answers.

- **Navigation Apps**

When Google Maps reroutes you around traffic, it's using AI to predict road conditions and estimate the fastest path.

- **Email Filters**

When spam gets caught before it reaches your inbox, AI is at work. It recognizes suspicious patterns and filters them out.

The point is simple: AI isn't just something "out there" in research labs.

It's already a silent partner in your daily routines. The difference now is that tools like ChatGPT and others have made AI visible and accessible, something you can interact with directly.

Story: The Hidden Helper

Let's go back to Paul, my neighbor.

A week after our conversation, he knocked on my door, looking sheepish.

"Okay," he said, "I think I've been using AI longer than I thought."

He explained that his doctor's office had called about a new prescription, and before he could ask, the pharmacist already knew his insurance coverage and co-pay.

"They said the system handled it automatically. That's AI, isn't it?"

It was.

"Then maybe it's not so scary after all," Paul admitted. "It's already helping me, and I didn't even know it."

That realization changed everything for him. And it can for you, too.

Reflection: Spot the AI in Your Day

Here's a quick exercise.

Take a moment and think about your last 24 hours. Where might AI have quietly shown up?

- Did your email filter out spam?
- Did your phone autocorrect a word?
- Did you stream a movie or listen to music?
- Did you check the weather forecast?

Write down five moments in your day where AI might have touched your life.

When you see it written out, you'll notice something important: AI isn't a faraway, intimidating invention.

It's already part of your everyday world. The question isn't whether you'll use it.

It's whether you'll learn to use it on purpose.

AI Is Not Magic

One reason AI feels intimidating is that people talk about it as if it's magical. It seems to "know" everything.

It produces answers instantly. It can even generate art or music.

But let's be clear: AI is not a wizard. It's not alive. It's not "thinking" in the way you think.

Here's a comparison that helps:

When a pianist sits at a piano, the instrument produces beautiful music. But the piano doesn't "know" music.

It only works when someone plays it.

When AI produces text, images, or sound, it looks impressive. But it doesn't "know" truth or meaning.

It only works because it has been trained to recognize patterns.

What feels magical is really mathematics at high speed.

Understanding this point is powerful. It helps you see AI as a tool, not as a replacement for your judgment.

The Strengths of AI

AI is remarkably good at certain things:

- Speed: It can process millions of data points in seconds.

  Imagine trying to read a thousand articles. AI can scan, summarize, and organize them in the time it takes you to sip your coffee.

- Consistency AI doesn't get tired. It doesn't lose focus after a long day.

  If you ask it to repeat a task 100 times, it will perform with the same energy every time.

- Pattern Recognition AI is excellent at spotting trends in messy data.

  That's why it's useful in detecting fraud, predicting weather, or even scanning medical images.

- Creativity by Combination AI can generate new recipes, songs, or designs by mixing patterns it has learned.

It doesn't "imagine" the way humans do, but it can remix existing knowledge into something fresh.

The Blind Spots of AI

For all its strengths, AI has weaknesses that are important to understand:

- No Common-Sense AI can't "understand" the way humans do.

If you asked it to write instructions for making a sandwich, it might forget to mention taking the bread out of the bag.

- No Judgment. It doesn't know what's appropriate or wise in context.

AI might generate a letter that sounds polite but sends the wrong message for your situation.

- Biased by Data AI learns from the information it's given.

If that data is biased, incomplete, or flawed, the output will reflect those flaws.

- Confidently Wrong AI can present false information with total confidence.

It doesn't "know" what's true; it predicts what words often appear together.

That can lead to convincing but inaccurate answers.

Why Humans Still Matter

This brings us to an essential truth: AI is only as good as the humans guiding it.

- **You provide the questions.** AI doesn't know what matters to you until you ask.
- **You provide the judgment.** AI can give you options, but only you can decide which fits your values and goals.
- You provide the meaning. AI can generate words, but only you give those words purpose.

Think of AI as a student who writes essays quickly. Some essays will be good, others sloppy.

You are the teacher, guiding, correcting, and deciding what's useful.

This means that instead of fearing replacement, you should focus on becoming the director of AI, not its servant.

Story: The Doctor and the Scan

A radiologist once told me about AI tools that scan medical images for signs of disease.

"The AI can spot patterns in scans faster than I can," she said.

"But it doesn't know which patterns are dangerous in the real world."

She explained that the AI might highlight an unusual shadow on an X-ray.

That's useful.

But it takes a human doctor to decide whether the shadow is cancer, scar tissue, or just the way the patient was positioned.

"The AI is a flashlight," she told me. "It shows me where to look. But I'm the one holding the map."

That's exactly how you should think of AI: a flashlight that helps you see more clearly, but never a replacement for your judgment.

Guided Exercise: AI's Strengths and Your Strengths

Take out a sheet of paper. Draw two columns. Label the left column "AI is good at" and the right column "I am good at."

In the left column, list what AI does well:

- Speed
- Consistency
- Spotting patterns
- Generating drafts

In the right column, list what you do well:

- Judgment
- Creativity with meaning
- Relationships and empathy
- Understanding context

Now, draw lines connecting the two columns where they can complement each other. For example:

- AI can draft a letter quickly → I can edit it to make sure it sounds like **me**.
- AI can summarize medical research → I can decide what it means for my life and family.
- AI can generate meal ideas → I can choose based on taste, culture, and preference.

This exercise shows you a simple truth: you don't compete with AI. You collaborate with it.

Sidebar: A Cautionary Tale

A man once asked an AI to give him investment advice.

It produced a very convincing summary of stocks to buy.

He nearly acted on it until he realized some of the companies didn't even exist.

AI can sound right without being right. That's why your role as a checker, guide, and decision-maker is so important.

The takeaway: Never hand over your full trust. Use AI as a partner, not a boss.

Human + AI in Daily Life

Imagine AI as a new coworker, eager, quick, and willing to take on the busywork.

But like a new employee, it needs direction. Without your input, it flounders. With your guidance, it shines.

Here's what that looks like in everyday life:

- Writing Letters AI can draft a thoughtful thank-you note in seconds.

  But only you know the tone, the inside jokes, or the warmth you want to add.

- Meal Planning AI can generate a week's worth of recipes.

  But only you know which foods your family actually enjoys and which ones cause an allergic reaction.

- Learning New Topics: AI can explain complex ideas in plain English.

  But only you decide which ones matter enough to pursue.

- Organizing Your Day: AI can build a daily schedule. But only you know your priorities, your energy levels, and your commitments.

  The pattern is always the same: AI does the fast draft, the quick prediction, the first version.

You provide the wisdom, the finishing touch, the decision.

Practical Prompts to Try

The easiest way to start is to simply ask AI questions in plain language.
Here are a few prompts you can try today:

- **For everyday life:** "Plan three easy dinners this week using chicken, rice, and vegetables. "Summarize this news article in five bullet points."
- **For learning:** "Explain the basics of climate change in simple terms. "Teach me the history of jazz like I'm a beginner."
- **For creativity:** "Write a lighthearted poem for my friend's birthday. "Give me five ideas for a family reunion theme."
- For organization: "Create a to-do list for hosting Thanksgiving dinner. "Draft a polite email asking my neighbor to trim their tree."

Think of prompts as conversation starters. You don't need to be formal or precise. Just ask.

If the answer isn't what you want, ask again in a different way. AI learns from your direction.

Story: Linda's Weekly Planner

Linda was overwhelmed. Between volunteer work, doctor appointments, and helping her grandchildren, she struggled to keep her week organized.
A friend suggested she try AI.

Skeptical, Linda typed: Create a weekly schedule for me.

I need three afternoons free for volunteering, two mornings for errands, and evenings for family time.

In seconds, she had a neat plan laid out. She adjusted it, swapping a few time slots, but the foundation was there.

"It's like having a personal assistant who actually listens," she said.

AI didn't run her life; it simply gave her a starting point she could shape.

Reflection: Spotting the Partnership

Take a sheet of paper. Write down three tasks in your life that feel repetitive or draining. Then, ask yourself:

- Could AI draft this for me?
- Could AI organize this for me?
- Could AI simplify this for me?

Now, write three tasks that require your heart, your wisdom, or your creativity.

Compare the lists. You'll notice something important: the first list is where AI can support you, while the second is where you remain irreplaceable.

This reflection makes the partnership clear. AI handles the routine. You handle the meaningful.

The Fear of Losing Humanity

Some people worry: If I use AI too much, will I lose what makes me human?

It's a fair concern. But history shows us the opposite.

- When calculators arrived, people didn't lose math skills; they used their freed-up time to focus on problem-solving. When washing machines arrived, people didn't lose the ability to clean clothes; they gained hours of their lives back.

AI won't erase your humanity. It highlights it. By offloading the repetitive tasks, you can invest more energy in relationships, creativity, and meaning.

Closing Summary: Plain and Simple

Here's what you need to remember from this chapter:

- **AI isn't magic.** It's a pattern machine, not a mind.
- **AI has strengths.** Speed, consistency, pattern recognition.
- **AI has blind spots.** No judgment, no common sense, no values.
- **You still matter.** Your wisdom, empathy, and judgment are irreplaceable.
- The partnership is the point. AI drafts; you direct. AI predicts; you decide.

If Chapter 1 was about fear, and Chapter 2 was about history, this chapter is about clarity.

You now know what AI is, and what it isn't.

You've seen how it already shows up in your life. And you've practiced seeing where AI ends, and you begin.

You don't need to understand the algorithms. You don't need to master the science.

You just need to remember: AI is a tool. And tools are meant to be picked up, used, and guided.

With that perspective, you're ready to move from understanding AI to actually working alongside it.

In the next chapter, we'll talk about what it means to treat AI as your personal copilot, not your replacement, but your helper.

Chapter 4: Your Life with a Copilot

A New Kind of Assistant

Janice never thought she'd have an assistant. She worked as a school secretary for years, balancing schedules, typing letters, and organizing events.

Now retired, she often joked, "I've always been the helper, never the one with help."

Then her son showed her ChatGPT.

"Think of it as your assistant," he said. "Ask it to help plan your week."

Skeptical, Janice typed: Make a weekly schedule for me.

I want time for morning walks, two afternoons for volunteering, and evenings for family calls.

In seconds, the AI produced a draft. It wasn't perfect; sometimes it didn't fit her routine, but it was a starting point.

She smiled. "It's like having a secretary again," she said, "but this time for me."

That's the essence of AI as a copilot. It's not here to take over.

It's here to ride alongside you, lighten your load, and help you focus on what matters most.

Helper, Not Replacement

A copilot doesn't fly the plane alone. The pilot sets the direction, makes the big decisions, and stays in control.

The copilot supports handling navigation, checklists, and communication.

That's how you should think of AI: as your copilot.

You remain the pilot of your life.

AI takes on the support roles.

Together, you fly farther and with less stress.

This mindset shift is critical. If you expect AI to be perfect, you'll be disappointed.

If you expect it to replace you, you'll feel threatened.

But if you expect it to assist, you'll find it powerful.

Everyday Examples of a Copilot at Work

So, what does "AI as copilot" actually look like? Here are a few examples:

- **Example 1: Writing Assistance**

  Need to draft a thank-you note? A job application cover letter? A tricky message to a friend?

  AI can create a draft in seconds. You then edit it to sound like you.

  Copilot role: Produces the draft. Your role: Add warmth, context, and final judgment.

- **Example 2: Scheduling and Planning**

  Overwhelmed by a big event, a birthday, reunion, or holiday dinner?

  Ask AI to create a timeline, to-do list, and even menu ideas.

  Copilot role: Suggests a structure. Your role: Approve, adjust, and personalize.

- **Example 3: Learning and Explaining**

  Confused by a medical term or financial concept? Ask AI to explain it "like I'm 10 years old."

  Suddenly, the fog clears.

  Copilot role: Breaks down complexity. Your role: Decide what matters to you.

- **Example 4: Travel Planning**

Want to take a road trip? Tell AI your starting point, budget, and interests.

It will suggest routes, stops, and attractions.

Copilot role: Provides options. Your role: Choose what excites you.

Story: Paul's Garden Plan

Paul loved gardening but hated the planning. He would buy seeds on impulse, then find himself with mismatched plants.

His daughter suggested he try AI.

He typed: Create a spring garden plan for me.

I live in North Carolina, have partial shade, and want vegetables and flowers together.

The AI generated a layout with tomatoes, lettuce, marigolds, and petunias.

Paul adjusted the list, but for the first time, he had a structured plan.

"It's like having a gardener's assistant," he said.

The garden flourished. And so did Paul's confidence.

The P.A.T.H. Method

One of the biggest misconceptions about AI is that you need to know the "right" words, like some secret password, to make it work.

In reality, you just need a little structure.

That's why I teach the P.A.T.H. Method, a four-step way to think about asking AI for help.

P.A.T.H. stands for:

- **P**rompt: Tell it what you want.
- **A**dd context, provide details to guide it.
- **T**ry again. Don't expect perfection on the first try.

- **H**andoff: You finish the job with your own judgment.

Let's break it down.

- P = Prompt

Start simple. A prompt is just a request.

Examples:

  - "Write a packing list for a three-day beach trip."
  - "Explain the difference between Medicare and Medicaid in simple terms."
  - "Create a poem for my granddaughter's birthday."

  The key is not to overthink it. Talk to the AI like you'd talk to a helpful assistant.

- A = Add Context

The more details you give, the better the results.

Instead of:

"Write a packing list."

Try:

"Write a packing list for a three-day beach trip for a family of four, including two small children."

Context sharpens the output.

- T = Try Again

AI doesn't get it right every time. That's okay. Treat it like a conversation.

If the first result isn't what you want, say:

  - "Make it shorter."
  - "Add more humor."
  - "Focus on healthy snacks."

Each time, the AI will adjust.

- H = Handoff

AI produces drafts. You provide the finishing touch.

  - Maybe it suggests a recipe, you add your family's secret seasoning. Maybe it writes a letter, you add your personal tone and story. Maybe it makes a schedule, you rearrange to match your energy levels.

  The handoff is where you turn the AI's draft into something that feels like you.

Story: The Family Reunion Letter

Let's see P.A.T.H. in action.

Barbara needed to write a letter inviting relatives to a family reunion. She didn't know where to start.

She typed: Write an invitation for a family reunion in July.

The AI gave her a basic draft. Nice, but too generic.

So, she added context: Make it warm and playful.

Mention that it's in Nashville, with music, food, and games for kids.

Now the letter sounded inviting, but a little too long.

She asked: Make it half as long and add a touch of humor.

Perfect. Barbara then did the handoff; she added a family joke and her own signature.

The result: a heartfelt, funny letter that sounded like Barbara, not a machine.

Her relatives loved it. "That's so you," one cousin said. And it was.

Step-by-Step Tutorial

Let's practice together.

- **Step 1:** Start with a simple prompt. Type: *Make a grocery list.*
- **Step 2:** Add context. Type: *Make a grocery list for five dinners this week, with easy recipes that cost under $15 per meal.*
- Step 3: Try again. If it gives meals you don't like, type: Replace fish with chicken.

  Add one vegetarian option.
- Step 4: Handoff. Take the final list and circle the meals your family will actually eat.

  Cross off the ones that don't fit your taste. Add your favorite recipe.

  Now the list is yours.

Guided Exercise: Your First Three Prompts

Take out your notebook. Write down three tasks from your life that feel like busywork or chores. Examples:

- Drafting an email.
- Planning a trip.
- Organizing a weekly schedule.

Now, for each task, write a P.A.T.H. prompt you could give to AI.

Example:

Task: Planning a trip.

Prompt: Plan a three-day trip to the mountains for two adults who like hiking and photography, with a budget of $500.

Try each one. Notice how AI responds. Then refine your prompt with more context. Adjust until it feels right.

Finally, add your own judgment to finish the task.

Congratulations, you've just used AI as your copilot.

Sidebar: The Confidence Builder

Many people freeze at the keyboard, thinking, what if I ask the wrong thing?

Here's the secret: there is no wrong thing.

The AI doesn't judge you. It doesn't laugh. It doesn't scold. It simply tries again.

That's why experimenting is the fastest way to build confidence.

Every prompt is practice. Every prompt makes you better.

Case Studies: A Copilot in Action

- **Case Study 1: The Retired Nurse**

Elaine, a retired nurse, struggled with the endless paperwork required to manage her husband's medical care.

Insurance forms, appointment reminders, and medication schedules were overwhelming.

Her daughter suggested she use AI to help. At first, Elaine resisted.

"I spent my whole career filling out charts," she said.

"I don't need a machine telling me what to do now."

But one day, out of frustration, she typed into an AI tool: Make a medication schedule for someone taking these prescriptions: one blood pressure pill in the morning, one cholesterol pill at night, and a multivitamin after lunch.

The AI produced a clear, color-coded schedule with reminders. Elaine adjusted it, printed it out, and taped it to the fridge.

"It doesn't replace my knowledge," she admitted, "but it makes me feel like I have backup."

Her fear of being controlled by the machine melted into gratitude for having a copilot by her side.

- **Case Study 2: The Small Business Owner**

Marcus ran a home repair business. He was great with tools, but not with words.

Advertising always felt like a struggle. "I can fix a roof," he said, "but I can't write a catchy ad."

A friend showed him how AI could help. Marcus typed: Write a friendly ad for a local handyman service.

Emphasize reliability, affordable rates, and same-day service for small jobs.

The AI delivered three versions. Marcus picked one, added his phone number, and put it in the community bulletin.

Within a week, he had three new customers.

"It's like having a marketing assistant who never sleeps," Marcus said. "I'm still the face of my business. But now I have help with the words."

- **Case Study 3: The Grandparent Storyteller**

Ruth loved telling stories to her grandchildren, but often ran out of ideas.

She asked AI: Write a bedtime story about a rabbit who wants to fly.

The AI created a short tale about a rabbit who builds wings from feathers.

Ruth added her own twists, adding names of the grandchildren as characters. The kids loved it.

"AI doesn't take away my role as the storyteller," Ruth said. "It just gives me a spark."

That spark rekindled her creativity. Instead of fearing AI, she now sees it as a partner in joy.

Reflection Exercise: My Copilot Opportunities

Take out your notebook. Write down five tasks you do regularly that feel like chores. Examples might include:

- Drafting grocery lists
- Writing emails
- Planning appointments
- Summarizing news articles
- Creating reminders

Next to each, write: How could AI act as my copilot here?

Example:

Task: Grocery list.

Copilot role: Suggest meals, organize the list by aisle.

My role: Add favorites, remove foods I don't like.

Once you complete your list, choose one task this week where you'll let AI be your copilot.

The goal isn't to automate your whole life. The goal is to learn the rhythm of partnership: draft, adjust, approve.

A Word on Trust

Some people hesitate to let AI help because they fear becoming too dependent.

"What if I forget how to do things myself?"

Here's the reassurance: AI won't erase your skills. It's no different than using a calculator, a spellchecker, or a GPS.

You still know how to add, spell, or read a map.

You just don't need to do it manually every time.

Trust isn't about giving up control. It's about allowing support while keeping your judgment intact.

You remain the pilot. AI is simply riding along.

Closing Summary: A Copilot for Life

At the start of this chapter, Janice discovered what it felt like to have an assistant for the first time.

By the end, she wasn't just smiling at the novelty; she was relying on AI as a partner in her daily life.

That's what AI as a copilot means:

- It doesn't replace you.
- It doesn't dictate your life.
- It supports, drafts, suggests, and reminds.

You set the direction. You choose the destination. AI simply helps you get there with less stress and more clarity.

Fear comes from believing you're on your own. Relief comes from realizing you have a copilot.

So as you move forward, remember this: you don't have to do everything by yourself anymore.

AI is ready to help, right now, today, with simple tasks that make your life lighter.

In the next chapter, we'll explore an equally important topic: how to protect yourself in the AI era, guarding your data, spotting scams, and using AI not only as a helper, but as a shield.

Chapter 5: Protecting Yourself in the AI Era

The New Risks We Face

The Scam Call

It started with a phone call. "Grandma, it's me. I need help. I'm in trouble." The voice sounded just like her grandson's. Panicked, she nearly sent money before realizing it was a scam.

The "voice" wasn't him at all; it was an AI-generated imitation.

This is one of the darker sides of artificial intelligence: criminals can use it too.

They can fake voices, photos, and even videos. They can write scam emails so polished that they look official.

That's why protecting yourself matters more than ever.

The Threat Landscape

AI brings incredible opportunities, but also new risks. Here are the main dangers to be aware of:

- Scams and Deepfakes Criminals can mimic voices, faces, and writing styles.

  Fake videos and audio recordings can be convincing enough to fool anyone.
- **Misinformation:** AI can generate articles, posts, or news stories that sound real but are completely false.
- **Privacy Leaks:** If you share too much personal information with AI tools, that data could be stored or misused. Be cautious about what personal details, photos, and voice samples you share online, as these contribute to data that can be used to generate convincing imitations.[3]

- Over-Reliance and Hallucination Risk If you let AI do your thinking for you, you risk losing your ability to judge what's real and what isn't. Because AI is a pattern predictor and can be "confidently wrong," you must never abdicate your human judgment for high-stakes information (medical diagnoses, legal advice, financial investments). The core message is that AI serves as a partner in gathering and organizing information, but human verification remains the ultimate, non-negotiable step.

The risks are real. But just like we adapted to phishing emails, password theft, and credit card fraud, we can adapt to these too.

Story: The Fake Email

Tom received an email that looked like it came from his bank.

It had the logo, the right colors, and a warning: "Your account has been locked. Click here to fix it."

He almost clicked, but something felt off. He called the bank instead. They confirmed it was fake.

The email had been written by AI, designed to trick him.

That moment taught Tom a valuable lesson: trust, but verify.

Why Awareness is Power

The first step to protecting yourself is awareness. Once you know the tricks, they lose much of their power.

Think of scams like stage magic. If you don't know how the illusion works, it feels dangerous.

But once you learn the trick, you can smile and say, "Not today."

The same is true of AI scams. Knowledge is your shield.

The Basics of Digital Safety

You don't need to become a cybersecurity expert. You just need a few habits that protect you from most threats.

- **Multi-Factor Authentication (2FA)** Implementing 2FA on all critical accounts (email, banking) provides a second layer of defense, mitigating up to 90 percent of account hacks, even if a scammer acquires the password.[3]
- **Share with Care** Be mindful of the personal data you share online, recognizing that details, photos, and voice samples contribute to the corpus of data that can be used to generate convincing imitations.[3]
- **Think Before You Click.** If a link or attachment looks suspicious, don't click. Verify with the source first.

The Deepfake Detection Checklist

For mitigating audio and video deepfake attempts, specific physical and auditory inconsistencies can serve as key indicators. Since these threats prey on trust and urgency, the first step in protection is heightened awareness and skepticism.

Red Flag	What to Look For	Action to Take
Visual Inconsistency	Unnatural or erratic blinking, misaligned lighting, or blurred edges around the face.[1]	Hang up or close the video. Do not proceed until verified.
Auditory Oddness	Flat tone, robotic cadence, or inconsistent speech patterns.[1]	Use a pre-arranged "safety word" or code phrase.
Urgency and Payment	Immediate need for money transfer, gift cards, or secret information (bank or SSN).	Pause. Verify the story/request by calling the person back on a known, trusted number.
Lack of 2FA	Any account lacking Two-Factor Authentication	Set up 2FA immediately on all critical accounts (email, bank).

Using AI to Stay Safe

Ironically, AI can also protect you from AI-powered scams.

- **Email Scams:** Some AI tools can scan emails and flag suspicious ones.

- **Fake News:** AI fact-checkers can compare claims against trusted sources.
- Password Security: AI can help you test the strength of your passwords.

AI is both the sword and the shield. The key is knowing how to wield it.

Exercise: My Personal Security Audit

Take a piece of paper and write down the following:

1. Do I use strong, unique passwords?
2. Do I use two-factor authentication?
3. Do I click links without checking?
4. Do I overshare online?

Score yourself honestly. Wherever you find a weak spot, choose one small step this week to improve it.

Example: If you don't use 2FA, set it up on your email account today. That one step can prevent 90% of account hacks.

Story: Ellen's Safety Net

Ellen once fell for a scam email that cost her $200.

Determined not to let it happen again, she used an AI-powered email filter.

The next time a scammer tried, the AI flagged the message instantly.

"It felt like having a guard dog watching my inbox," she said.

Technology may create risks, but it also provides tools to protect ourselves.

Why Fear Doesn't Help

Fear can make you freeze. You hear about scams, deepfakes, and privacy risks, and you think, Maybe I should avoid AI altogether.

But avoidance is the real danger. By staying away, you not only miss the benefits, but you also leave yourself more vulnerable because you're uninformed.

The goal isn't to fear AI. The goal is to use it wisely.

Reflection: What Is My Data Worth?

Take a moment to reflect. Your data, your personal information, photos, health details, and financial records are valuable.

Companies and scammers alike want it.

Write down:

1. What data do I want to keep private?
2. Who do I trust with that data?
3. What steps will I take to protect it?

This reflection shifts your mindset from vague worry to concrete action.

Story: Robert's Calm Confidence

Robert used to panic whenever he heard about identity theft.

But after setting up stronger passwords, enabling 2FA, and using AI to scan his emails, he felt different.

"I'm not scared anymore," he said. "I'm prepared."

That's the power of confidence. It doesn't come from pretending the risks don't exist.

It comes from knowing you have a plan.

Closing Summary: Safety First

Here's the bottom line:

- AI introduces new risks, but also new protections.
- Scams and deepfakes can be frightening, but awareness make them weaker.
- Simple habits, strong passwords, 2FA, and caution with links, protect you from most threats.
- AI itself can be your ally, acting as a shield against fraud and misinformation.

You don't need to fear AI. You just need to respect it.

Think of it like fire: dangerous if uncontrolled, but incredibly useful when managed wisely.

With your safety net in place, you're free to explore AI with less anxiety and more curiosity.

And that's exactly what we'll do in the next chapter, discovering how AI can make learning easier, faster, and even fun.

Chapter 6: Learning Made Easy

The Joy of Learning Again

The Piano Story

When George retired, he decided to take up the piano. He had always loved music, but never had the chance to learn.

After two frustrating weeks of practicing scales, he sighed, "Maybe I'm just too old for this."

His granddaughter, who was learning coding at school, suggested, "Why don't you ask AI to be your music tutor?"

Skeptical, George typed into an AI tool: Teach me piano basics in 15-minute lessons, three times a week.

Make it fun and simple.

The AI responded with a clear plan: short warm-ups, easy songs, tips for hand positioning. George followed the steps.

A month later, he was playing a tune recognizable enough that his wife sang along.

George laughed, shaking his head. "I thought the hard part was my age. Turns out the hard part was not having a guide."

That's what AI can be: a patient, tireless tutor who adjusts to your pace.

The Myth: "I'm Too Old to Learn"

This myth runs deep. Many people believe that after a certain age, the brain can't adapt. But science says otherwise.

Your brain has something called neuroplasticity, the ability to form new connections at any age.

It may take longer to master certain skills, but learning is always possible.

The real obstacle isn't your brain. It's fear, impatience, or lack of guidance. AI helps by breaking learning into bite-sized steps, available whenever you want, without judgment.

No sighs, no rolled eyes, no, "You should already know this." Just patient guidance.

Why AI Makes Learning Easier

Here's what makes AI uniquely suited as a tutor:

- **Personalized Pacing:** It doesn't care if you want to repeat the same lesson five times.
- **Plain Language**: You can ask, "Explain this like I'm five," and it will.
- **Endless Patience:** It never gets tired of your questions.
- **Variety:** It can teach through text, quizzes, practice exercises, or even games.
- **Availability:** It's there whenever you're curious, morning, midnight, or in between.

Story: Maria Learns Italian

Maria had always wanted to learn Italian, so she could connect with her grandparents' heritage.

She had tried language apps but felt lost after a few lessons.

Then she asked AI: Teach me 10 Italian phrases I can use when traveling. Give me pronunciation tips and a practice quiz.

The AI delivered exactly that. Maria practiced daily, testing herself with the quizzes.

By the time she visited Rome, she could order food, ask for directions, and even chat briefly with locals.

"It wasn't perfect," she admitted, "but it was enough to make me feel connected. And that gave me joy."

Exercise: Pick a Skill

Take out your notebook. Write down one skill you've always wanted to learn but put off. It could be:

- A language
- A hobby (painting, photography, knitting)
- A practical skill (budgeting, cooking new cuisines)
- A digital skill (editing photos, using spreadsheets)

Now, write a simple AI prompt: Create a 7-day beginner's plan to learn [skill].

Make it easy, step by step, and encourage me along the way.

This is your first lesson plan. Try it this week.

The Wall We All Hit

If you've ever tried to learn something new, from knitting to driving a stick shift, you know about the wall.

It's the moment you think: This is too hard. I'll never get it.

For adults, that wall feels heavier. Children expect to stumble; adults often expect to succeed quickly.

So, when progress feels slow, frustration sets in.

AI can't erase frustration, but it can help you move through it with less pain.

Story: Peter and the Computer

Peter decided to learn basic coding. Two hours in, he muttered, "This is nonsense."

Instead of quitting, he asked AI: Why am I getting an error in this code? Explain it like I'm brand new.

The AI pointed out the missing punctuation and explained the rule.

Peter laughed. "So, I was tripping over a semicolon? I was ready to quit over that?"

Sometimes frustration comes from not knowing where you're stuck. AI shines a light on the exact spot, then helps you climb over it.

How AI Reinforces Learning

AI isn't just good for explaining. It's also excellent for reinforcing knowledge. Here's how:

- **Immediate Feedback** You can ask AI to quiz you, then check your answers instantly. No waiting for a teacher.
- **Customized Practice** If you struggle with one part of a subject, AI can drill you on just that until it sticks.
- **Encouragement** AI can even give positive reinforcement. "Great job! You nailed 8 out of 10 questions. Let's try again."
- Different Angles. If one explanation doesn't work, AI can re-explain the same concept five different ways.

Example: Cooking Skills

Let's say you're learning to cook Thai food. You try Pad Thai, but it turns out too salty.

Instead of giving up, you ask AI: Why did my Pad Thai turn out too salty, and how can I fix it next time?

The AI might explain the balance in Thai cooking: sweet, sour, salty, spicy.

Then it suggests: "Add more lime juice or a bit of sugar to balance the flavor."

Next attempt? Success.

AI reinforces your learning not by handing you a finished skill, but by helping you spot what went wrong and how to adjust.

The Emotional Boost of Progress

One of the most discouraging parts of learning is not knowing if you're making progress.

AI can help by measuring and celebrating small wins.

For example:

- *Teach me 10 Spanish words. Quiz me until I get them all right.*
- *Give me a 5-question test on budgeting basics.*
- Show me my progress over the last three sessions.

The sense of progress fuels motivation. You see yourself getting better, even in small steps, and that keeps you going.

Guided Exercise: AI as Your Coach

Let's try a practical exercise.

Pick a subject or skill you want to improve. Example: public speaking.

Write a prompt: Act as a coach and give me three short exercises to practice public speaking at home.

Follow the exercises. Maybe it suggests practicing a 1-minute speech in front of a mirror, recording yourself, and summarizing a news article aloud.

After completing them, ask AI: Give me feedback on how I can improve my delivery, clarity, and confidence.

Even though AI can't "see" you, it can give general tips and reminders. It keeps you moving instead of stalling.

Story: Joan and the Camera

Joan loved photography but was intimidated by the manual settings on her new camera.

She asked AI: Teach me the basics of aperture, shutter speed, and ISO in simple terms.

The AI explained using metaphors: aperture is the eye's pupil, shutter speed is how fast the eyelid blinks, and ISO is the eye's sensitivity to light.

Joan finally understood. She asked: Give me five practice exercises I can do with my camera to master these settings.

Each week, she tried them. Within a month, she was confidently shooting family portraits and nature scenes.

"The camera used to scare me," Joan said. "Now it feels like an extension of my eye."

Why This Matters

When learning feels easier, you're more likely to keep going.

AI doesn't just provide information; it makes the process less lonely, less frustrating, and more encouraging.

It's like having a tutor who is always available, never impatient, and happy to explain things again and again until you get it.

Learning as Joy, Not Obligation

When we were children, learning felt natural. We chased butterflies, asked endless questions, and soaked up stories.

Somewhere along the way, though, learning turned into tests, grades, and pressure.

For many adults, the word "learning" feels heavy. It's tied to classrooms, deadlines, and the fear of failing.

AI can help us rediscover the lighter side of learning, the curiosity, the play, and the sense of delight in discovering something new.

Story: Frank and the Stars

Frank had always loved looking at the night sky, but astronomy books felt overwhelming. Too many charts, too much math.

One night, he asked AI: Teach me to recognize five constellations I can see from my backyard in Florida.

Explain like I'm a beginner, and tell me a story about each one.

The AI described Orion, Cassiopeia, and others, complete with myths and simple diagrams.

Frank went outside, looked up, and spotted his first constellation.

"It was like meeting old friends in the sky," he said. "I felt ten years old again."

That joy is what learning can be when pressure is removed.

The Legacy of Lifelong Learning

Learning isn't just about gaining new skills. It's about staying mentally sharp, emotionally engaged, and spiritually alive.

Studies show that people who continue to learn as they age experience:

- Better memory retention
- Lower risk of cognitive decline
- Greater sense of purpose and satisfaction

But beyond science, there's something deeper. Lifelong learning lets you leave a legacy.

It shows your children and grandchildren that curiosity never ends.

When they see you trying new things, they learn that growth has no expiration date.

Story: Helen's Family Cookbook

Helen always wanted to write a cookbook of family recipes, but didn't know how to structure it.

She asked AI: Help me organize a family cookbook with 20 recipes. Include space for stories and photos.

The AI provided a clear outline: sections by meal type, notes for personal memories, and ideas for layout.

Helen added her own touches, handwritten anecdotes, old photographs, and stories about holiday traditions.

When she gave copies to her grandchildren, they were amazed.

"This isn't just food," one said. "It's our history."

Helen smiled. AI had given her the framework, but the soul of the cookbook came from her heart.

That's what lifelong learning does: it turns knowledge into legacy.

Reflection Exercise: What Would I Love to Learn?

Take a quiet moment. Ask yourself:

1. If difficulty didn't matter, what would I love to learn?
2. What skill or subject has always sparked my curiosity?
3. How could learning it bring joy or meaning into my life now?

Write down your answers. Don't judge them. Don't say, "I'm too old" or "That's not practical."

Maybe it's painting. Maybe it's learning guitar. Maybe it's exploring family history.

Then, write a simple AI prompt: Create a beginner's plan to learn [skill/subject].

Make it step by step, fun, and suited for someone just starting.

This reflection is your first step toward joy-driven learning.

Story: Charles and the Harmonica

Charles found an old harmonica in his attic. He had never played before but was curious.

He asked AI: Teach me three simple songs I can play on the harmonica in one week.

The AI suggested "Twinkle, Twinkle," "Oh Susanna," and "Amazing Grace." It gave him step-by-step instructions.

A week later, Charles was playing tunes for his friends.

"It wasn't Carnegie Hall," he laughed, "but it was fun. And fun was enough."

Learning doesn't need to be grand. It just needs to bring joy.

Closing Summary: Curiosity Is the Compass

Here's what we've discovered in this chapter:

- The myth of being "too old to learn" is false. Your brain is capable of growth at any age.
- AI is a patient, personalized tutor that adapts to your pace and needs.
- Frustration is normal, but AI helps you push through by pinpointing errors, offering feedback, and celebrating small wins.

- Learning can be joyful again, a chance to rediscover curiosity, not endure obligation.
- Every skill you pick up, every story you capture, every project you complete adds to your legacy.

Learning is not just about adding information. It's about expanding possibilities, keeping your spirit alive, and showing the next generation that curiosity is ageless.

With AI as your tutor, the classroom is always open, the lessons are always patient, and the joy of discovery is always within reach.

In the next chapter, we'll move from learning to living more efficiently, exploring how AI can save you time on everyday tasks, so you can spend your energy on the things that truly matter.

Chapter 7: Everyday Time Savers

Why Time Matters More Than Ever

The Gift of Time

When Sarah retired, she thought her days would slow down.

Instead, she found herself busier than ever, juggling errands, volunteering, babysitting grandchildren, and managing the household.

One morning, she sighed, "I thought retirement meant free time, but I feel like I'm always behind."

That's where AI comes in. Its greatest gift isn't just knowledge, it's time.

By offloading small tasks, it frees hours that you can spend on joy, connection, and rest.

The Myth of Busyness

We often treat busyness like a badge of honor. "I'm so busy," we say, as if that means we're valuable.

But busyness often crowds out the things that matter most.

AI can help shift that balance. It won't eliminate responsibilities, but it can cut down the time spent on repetitive or draining ones.

Think of AI as your time-saving partner, like a dishwasher for your mind.

Everyday Tasks That Eat Time

Here are a few common time drains:

- Writing repetitive emails
- Planning meals and grocery lists
- Organizing appointments
- Searching for information
- Summarizing long articles or documents

- Drafting schedules and to-do lists

Each of these can take 10–30 minutes. AI can shrink that to 2–3 minutes.

Story: David's Doctor Appointments

David was managing his wife's medical care and often felt buried in paperwork.

One evening, he typed into an AI tool: Organize these five doctors' appointments into a clear schedule with reminders.

Include travel times and what paperwork I need to bring.

In seconds, he had a neat calendar with everything in order.

"It felt like hiring a personal assistant for free," he said.

"Instead of shuffling papers, I could focus on being present with my wife."

Why Time-Saving Matters at This Stage of Life

At this point in life, time feels more precious than ever. You've worked hard, built relationships, and faced challenges.

The last thing you need is to waste hours on chores a machine can handle.

AI won't add more hours to your day. But it can help you spend the hours you do have on the things that truly matter.

Reflection Exercise: Where Do I Lose Time?

Take a moment and think about your week. Where do you feel time slipping away?

Write down three tasks that drain your time. Examples:

- Writing the same kinds of emails over and over
- Planning meals from scratch every week
- Sorting through long articles for one piece of information

These are your prime candidates for AI support.

Practical Ways AI Saves Time

Now that we've looked at why time matters, let's get practical.

How can AI actually give you back hours each week?

1. Meal Planning and Grocery Lists

Cooking is one of life's daily joys, but planning meals and making grocery lists can feel like a chore.

With AI:

You can ask: Create a 7-day dinner plan for two adults, with recipes under 30 minutes, using chicken, fish, and vegetables.

AI will produce a plan, meals, recipes, and even a grocery list.

Instead of staring at the fridge wondering, "What's for dinner?" you already have a plan.

Story: Sharon's Weeknight Rescue Sharon dreaded the "what's for dinner" question. Every night, it sparked stress.

After trying AI, she said, "It was like someone had already thought it through for me. I didn't waste half an hour debating what to cook. That time went back to enjoying dinner with my husband."

2. Scheduling and Reminders

Missed appointments and forgotten tasks cause unnecessary stress. AI can build schedules and remind you of priorities.

With AI:

Prompt: Create a weekly schedule that includes two mornings for exercise, three afternoons for errands, and evenings for reading.

You can ask it to also add reminders for my dentist appointment and my granddaughter's recital.

The AI won't just remind you; it will organize your week around your real life.

3. Writing and Communication

Sometimes the hardest part of writing isn't the message itself, it's starting.

With AI:

Draft polite emails: *Write a polite email to my neighbor asking if we can discuss trimming the tree that hangs over my yard.*

Create thank-you notes: *Write a short, heartfelt thank-you note for a birthday gift of books.*

Summarize information: Summarize this article in five bullet points.

What used to take 20 minutes can take 2.

4. Research and Quick Answers

Instead of scrolling through websites or digging through books, AI can cut straight to the answer.

With AI:

- *Explain Medicare Part B in simple terms.*
- *What are the pros and cons of hybrid cars?*
- Summarize three common treatments for arthritis, including side effects.

It's like having a reference librarian available 24/7.

Caution: AI can sometimes provide outdated or inaccurate information.

Always double-check important answers, especially health or financial ones, with trusted sources.

Guided Exercise: Your "Time Thieves"

Take your notebook. Write the phrase: My three biggest time thieves are…

Examples might be:

- Planning meals
- Writing repetitive emails
- Sorting paperwork

Next, write a prompt for each one.

- **For meal planning:** *Make a grocery list for five healthy dinners under $15 each.*
- **For emails:** *Draft a polite email asking to reschedule an appointment.*
- For paperwork: Organize these five appointments into a clear weekly schedule with times and notes.

Try them this week. Notice how much time you save.

Even if each saves just 10–15 minutes, that's an hour or more back in your pocket.

Story: Linda's Hour a Day

Linda tracked her AI use for a month. Between meal planning, drafting emails, and organizing her calendar, she estimated she saved about an hour each day.

"That's seven hours a week," she said. "A whole workday! And instead of filling it with chores, I fill it with family."

That's the real gift of AI: time-saving, not just efficiency, but space for what matters.

From Chores to Choices

The Real Question

When AI saves you time, the question becomes: What will I do with it?

Because time saved isn't just about getting more done. It's about creating space for rest, for connection, for creativity, for joy.

You don't want to fill every freed-up minute with more busyness. You want to use it intentionally.

Case Studies: How People Used Their Time Savings

- Case Study 1: Evelyn the Volunteer

  Evelyn used AI to streamline her weekly church newsletter. Instead of typing announcements from scratch, she asked AI: Draft a church bulletin with service times, upcoming events, and a welcoming message.

  She edited and personalized it in minutes. What used to take her three hours now took one.

  What did she do with the extra two hours? She spent them visiting members who couldn't attend services in person.

"AI didn't just save me time," she said. "It gave me back relationships."

- **Case Study 2: Harold and His Garden**

Harold loved gardening but hated paperwork. He used AI to organize supply lists and track his seasonal planting.

With that time saved, he started teaching his grandkids about gardening.

"Before, I barely had energy to keep up," Harold explained.

"Now I can share my passion. That's better than any harvest."

- **Case Study 3: Denise's Daily Calm**

Denise was caring for her aging mother. She used AI to plan meals, create a medication schedule, and write reminder notes.

That shaved an hour off her daily routine.

"I finally had time to sit with my mom and just talk," she said.

"Those conversations mean more than any task list."

Reflection Exercise: My Freed-Up Time

Take out your notebook. Answer these questions:

1. If AI gave me back one hour a day, what would I want to do with it?
    - Rest?
    - Connect with family?
    - Pick up a hobby?
    - Volunteer?

2. How could I use that hour to improve my well-being, relationships, or joy?
3. What's one small change I could make this week to spend my reclaimed time with purpose?

The Trap to Avoid

Some people use the time AI saves just to cram in more chores. That's not the goal.

If AI helps you write emails faster, don't just write more emails; use the extra time to breathe, to walk, to call a friend.

Remember: the point isn't productivity. The point is freedom.

Story: Margaret's Afternoon Walks

Margaret always said she was "too busy" for exercise. After using AI to handle her weekly grocery planning and volunteer scheduling, she saved nearly five hours a week.

She decided to spend that time walking in the park each afternoon.

"I thought I was too busy," she said, "but I was really just stuck in chores. Now I feel healthier and happier."

Her walks became her favorite part of the day.

Closing Summary: Time Is Life

Here's what this chapter taught us:

- Time is your most precious resource.
- AI can take over repetitive tasks like meal planning, scheduling, writing, and research.
- Even small savings, 10 minutes here, 20 minutes there, add up to hours each week.

- The true value of AI time-saving isn't more busyness, but more freedom.

Imagine if you reclaimed an hour a day for the rest of your life.

That's 365 hours a year, more than 15 days. What could you do with that gift?

The answer is up to you. Rest. Connect. Create. Share. Laugh. Live.

AI doesn't just give you information. It gives you back your most precious resource: time.

And with more time in your hands, the next question is: how will you invest it in the people, passions, and priorities that matter most?

In the next chapter, we'll explore one of those investments, using AI to connect with others more deeply through letters, stories, and shared projects.

Chapter 8: Connecting with Others

Why Connection Matters Most

The Loneliness Problem

As people get older, one of the greatest challenges isn't physical health; it's loneliness.

Friends move, children get busy, communities shift. Sometimes health or mobility makes it harder to stay connected.

But connection is more than a luxury. Studies show it's as essential to well-being as exercise or diet.

People who maintain close connections live longer, healthier, and happier lives.

AI can't replace human love or companionship. But it can help you stay in touch, express yourself more easily, and keep relationships alive, especially when communication feels like a burden.

Story: Ann's Birthday Letters

Ann loved her grandchildren dearly but found it hard to keep up with birthdays.

She often worried her short notes felt too generic.

One day, she asked AI: Write a warm, funny birthday message for an 8-year-old boy who loves dinosaurs.

The AI delivered a playful note full of dinosaur jokes. Ann added a few personal touches and mailed it.

Her grandson laughed and told her, "Grandma, you're the funniest!"

Ann beamed. "AI didn't replace my love," she said. "It helped me express it better."

How AI Helps Communication

Here are some ways AI can support connection:

- Drafting Notes and Letters AI can create drafts for thank-you notes, invitations, or holiday letters.

  You edit to make it personal.

- **Translation:** If you have family or friends who speak another language, AI can translate your words so you can communicate more easily.

- **Storytelling** AI can help you capture family stories, polish them into readable drafts, and preserve them for future generations.

- **Memory Aids** AI can remind you of birthdays, anniversaries, and important dates, so loved ones feel remembered and valued.

Reflection: Where Do I Struggle with Connection?

Ask yourself:

1. Do I struggle to find the right words for letters or notes?
2. Do I forget important dates?
3. Do I want to capture family stories, but don't know how to start?

Wherever you feel stuck, AI can step in as your partner, not to replace your voice, but to amplify it.

Connecting with Others

Writing With Warmth

Sometimes the hardest part of staying connected is finding the words. A blank page feels intimidating.

You care deeply, but how do you say it?

AI can give you a starting point.

- **Thank-you notes:** *Write a warm thank-you note for a handmade scarf, mentioning how cozy it feels on winter walks.*
- **Holiday letters:** *Draft a cheerful holiday update from a family of four, highlighting travels, hobbies, and gratitude.*
- Condolence messages: Help me write a gentle sympathy note for a friend who lost her brother.

You don't have to send the AI's draft as-is. Instead, treat it as a foundation.

Add your personal details, your memories, your voice. The result is quicker, but also more thoughtful.

Remembering Special Dates

AI can act as a reminder service. You can feed it birthdays, anniversaries, and important milestones.

Then, instead of panicking the night before, you'll have a gentle nudge: Your granddaughter's recital is tomorrow, so maybe send her a note of encouragement.

These small touches mean a lot. A remembered birthday or a timely encouragement often carries more weight than grand gestures.

Translation for Connection

Imagine being able to send a note in Spanish to your neighbor, or in Italian to an extended relative, without worrying about mistakes.

Prompt: Translate this note into Spanish, keeping it friendly and casual: "Thank you for bringing over soup when I wasn't feeling well. It meant a lot."

Suddenly, language is no longer a barrier to connection.

Storytelling: Preserving Your Legacy

Beyond daily notes and reminders, AI can help with something deeper: preserving your family's history.

Your life is full of stories, moments of courage, lessons learned, funny mishaps, and traditions passed down.

Often, these stories fade because they aren't written down. AI can help you capture them.

Prompts to try:

- *Turn this memory into a short story: "When I was 10, my brother and I got lost in the woods but found our way home by following the sound of church bells."*
- *Help me write a family history chapter about moving into our first home in 1972.*
- Organize my notes about family recipes into a cookbook format with introductions and anecdotes.

AI acts as an editor and organizer, helping you shape memories into something future generations can treasure.

Story: Walter's War Letters

Walter had a box of letters he wrote home while serving in the military decades ago.

He wanted to preserve them but didn't know how.

He asked AI: Summarize these letters into a narrative that captures my experience, but keep the personal tone.

The AI created a flowing story from dozens of scattered letters.

Walter added details, corrected parts, and shared the finished story with his grandchildren.

"They finally understood what those years meant," Walter said. "And I finally felt like my story had been told."

Guided Exercise: Write and Share

Take out your notebook. Think of one person you'd like to reconnect with. It could be:

- A family member
- A friend you haven't spoken to in years
- A neighbor you'd like to know better

Now, write a simple AI prompt: Draft a short, warm message to reconnect with an old friend.

Mention how I've been thinking of them and would love to catch up over coffee.

Review the draft. Add your own touches. Send it.

Connection doesn't have to be complicated. Sometimes one message is all it takes to reopen a door.

Stories of Connection

- **Case Study 1: The Reunion Organizer**

Sam wanted to bring together his extended family, but the thought of planning overwhelmed him.

He asked AI: Create a plan for a family reunion in July for 30 people, including meals, games, and a schedule.

The AI gave him a framework: menus, activity ideas, and even sample invitation wording.

Sam added his own family traditions and sent the invitations.

His cousin said afterward, "That was the smoothest reunion we've ever had."

Sam laughed. "I didn't do it alone; I had a copilot."

- **Case Study 2: The Story Collector**

Marjorie loved hearing her mother's stories but worried they'd be lost.

She asked AI: Turn these voice recordings into a written family history, keeping the storytelling tone warm and personal.

The AI organized the transcripts into chapters. Marjorie added photos and anecdotes.

At Christmas, she presented a book to her children and grandchildren.

"It was more than a gift," she said. "It was a bridge between generations."

- **Case Study 3: The Caregiver's Notes**

James cared for his father, who was beginning to show signs of memory loss.

He wanted to keep the family updated, but found writing long updates exhausting.

He asked AI: Draft a weekly family update about Dad's health. Keep it clear, compassionate, and encouraging.

The AI gave him a draft he could tweak in minutes. Instead of dreading the updates, James sent them regularly.

Family members appreciated being included, and James felt less alone.

Reflection: Connection as Legacy

Think about your own life. When people remember you, what do you want them to say?

- "She was always there for me."
- "He made me laugh when I needed it."
- "They shared our family stories and kept them alive."

That's your legacy. AI can't create love, but it can help you express it, preserve it, and pass it on.

Take a moment and write in your notebook:

1. One person I want to reach out to this week is…
2. One story I want to capture for my family is…
3. One memory I want to share before it fades is…

These small actions, repeated, build a legacy of connection.

Story: Grace's Goodbye Gift

Grace knew her health was failing. She asked AI: Help me write letters to each of my grandchildren, sharing advice, love, and a special memory.

The AI drafted heartfelt letters, which Grace personalized with her own words. After her passing, the letters were delivered.

"They felt like she was still with us," one grandchild said.

Grace's legacy wasn't just the letters; it was the love she chose to leave behind, amplified by AI.

Closing Summary: Technology as a Bridge

Here's what we've seen in this chapter:

- Connection is the most valuable part of life.
- AI can support connection by helping with words, reminders,

translations, and storytelling.

- It doesn't replace love or presence; it amplifies them.
- The real gift of AI is not efficiency here, but intimacy: making it easier to stay close to the people who matter.

Technology is often accused of isolating us. But when used wisely, it can become a bridge.

It can make our love more visible, our stories more lasting, and our relationships more vibrant.

As you continue exploring AI, remember: its greatest power isn't in what it produces, but in what it preserves, your ability to connect, to share, and to love.

In the next chapter, we'll look at another essential part of thriving in the AI era: keeping your independence.

Chapter 9: Staying Independent

Independence Matters

The Fear of Losing Control

One of the deepest fears many people face as they get older is losing independence. Needing too much help.

Relying too much on others. Becoming a burden.

AI can't erase every challenge of aging or busy life, but it can help extend independence, not by replacing your decisions, but by supporting them.

Think of it this way: independence doesn't mean doing everything alone.

It means being able to live life on your terms. AI can help make that possible.

Story: Harold and the Medications

Harold took six different medications at different times of day.

He kept forgetting which pill came when, until one day he mixed them up.

His daughter worried.

At her suggestion, Harold asked AI: Create a daily medication schedule for six prescriptions, with reminders at the right times.

The AI generated a chart with colors and times. Harold taped it to his fridge and synced reminders to his phone.

"I still manage my health," Harold said. "I just have a smarter system now."

AI didn't take away his independence. It gave it back.

How AI Supports Daily Independence

Here are some practical ways AI can help people live more freely:

- **Health Management**
    - Creating medication schedules
    - Summarizing the doctor's instructions in plain English
    - Suggesting diet or exercise plans tailored to your needs
- **Household Organization**
    - Drafting shopping lists
    - Creating cleaning or maintenance checklists
    - Planning weekly schedules
- **Financial Clarity**
    - Summarizing bills
    - Creating simple budgets
    - Explaining confusing financial terms
- **Learning and Problem-Solving**
    - Explaining instructions (from recipes to tech manuals) in simple steps
    - Offering troubleshooting guides for household problems

Reflection: What Feels Harder Lately?

Take a moment. Ask yourself:

1. Are there daily tasks that feel more confusing than they used to?
2. Do you struggle to keep track of appointments, finances, or paperwork?
3. Where do you feel most at risk of losing independence?

Write down three of these areas. These are where AI can step in as your partner, helping you stay capable and in control.

Practical Tools for Independence

Health Support

Managing health is one of the biggest challenges to independence. Appointments, instructions, medications, it adds up quickly.

AI can ease the load.

- **Medication schedules:** *Create a daily medication chart for three prescriptions, one in the morning, one after lunch, and one before bed.*
- **Doctor's notes explained:** *Explain this medical report in plain English, focusing only on what actions I need to take.*
- Healthy meal plans: Suggest a 5-day meal plan for someone with diabetes, using easy recipes and affordable ingredients.

AI isn't a doctor. But it can act like a translator and organizer, turning complexity into clarity.

Story: Denise's Clarity Denise left her doctor's office with a packet of papers she didn't understand.

"It felt like another language," she admitted. She uploaded the notes to an AI tool and asked, Summarize this in plain English.

The AI gave her three clear steps: adjust medication, schedule a blood test, and change diet slightly.

"I finally felt like I knew what was going on," Denise said. That clarity restored her sense of control.

Financial Support

Money management can feel overwhelming with multiple bills, accounts, and confusing terms. AI can simplify.

- **Budgeting:** *Create a monthly budget for $3,000 income, covering rent, groceries, transportation, and savings.*
- **Bill organization:** *Organize these five bills into a calendar with due dates and amounts.*
- **Explaining terms:** *Explain compound interest in plain language with an example.*

Story: Carl's Confidence Carl prided himself on being independent with his finances, but new banking apps left him lost.

AI helped by generating step-by-step guides. "It was like having a patient tutor," Carl said.

"Now I handle my money without bothering my kids."

Safety and Security

Independence means feeling safe. AI can help here, too.

- **Scam detection:** *Ask AI, does this email look suspicious?*
- **Emergency prep:** *Create a step-by-step plan for what to do in case of a power outage.*
- Daily reminders: Remind me every night at 9 p.m. to lock the doors.

Small supports add up to peace of mind.

Mobility and Daily Living

Even if you're active, organizing transportation or errands can be time-consuming.

- **Trip planning:** *Plan a trip to the grocery store, pharmacy, and post office in the most efficient order.*
- **Exercise prompts:** *Suggest five light exercises I can do at home in 20 minutes to stay active.*
- **Local information:** *Find community events this weekend within 10 miles.*

Story: Eleanor's Outings Eleanor stopped driving at 78 but still wanted to attend community events.

She asked AI: List transportation options in my town for seniors, with costs and schedules.

Within minutes, she had a plan that gave her freedom again.

"I thought giving up the car meant giving up life," she said.

"Turns out, it meant finding new ways to get where I want to go."

Guided Exercise: My Independence Map

Take your notebook. Draw three columns:

Task I struggle with	**How AI could help**	**What I still control**
Remembering medications	Creates a schedule and reminders	Taking the pills and checking off each dose
Managing bills	Organizes due dates	Deciding when and how to pay
Planning meals	Suggests menus and shopping lists	Choosing recipes that fit my taste
This exercise shows that independence isn't lost when you accept help.		
It's strengthened because you stay in charge of the decisions.		

Real Stories of Independence

- **Case Study 1: Martin and the Bills**

Martin dreaded the first week of the month when all his bills came due.

He often paid late because he lost track of due dates.

He asked AI: Organize these bills, rent, electricity, phone, and insurance, into a monthly calendar with due dates and reminders.

The AI produced a clear table. Martin printed it out and taped it above his desk.

"For the first time in years, I wasn't late," Martin said proudly. "I don't feel helpless anymore. I feel capable."

- **Case Study 2: Paula and the Garden Tools**

Paula's eyesight was fading, and reading tool manuals was frustrating.

She asked AI: Explain how to assemble this gardening tool in simple steps, without jargon.

The AI rewrote the instructions clearly. Paula followed them and had the tool ready in under an hour.

"It wasn't about the tool," she said. "It was about not having to call my son for help with something small. That kept my dignity."

- **Case Study 3: Robert's Travel Plan**

Robert wanted to attend his niece's wedding but felt overwhelmed by planning the trip, flights, hotels, and transportation.

He asked AI: Plan a 3-day trip from Atlanta to Chicago for a wedding, budget $800, including a hotel near the venue.

The AI gave him a draft itinerary. Robert booked the trip himself, feeling empowered.

"I thought my traveling days were over," he said. "But AI gave me the confidence to go."

Reflection: Redefining Independence

Many people think independence means doing everything alone. But true independence means living on your terms, even if you use support.

A cane doesn't mean you're weak; it means you're strong enough to keep walking.

Glasses don't mean you've failed; they mean you want to keep seeing clearly.

AI doesn't mean you've given up control; it means you've found a tool to stay capable.

Independence isn't about avoiding help. It's about choosing the right kind of help that empowers you.

Reflection Exercise: My "AI and Me" Plan

Write down three areas where you want to stay independent. Examples:

- Managing health
- Handling finances
- Keeping up with family

Next to each, write one way AI could help. Then, write one way you remain in control.

Example:

- **Health:** AI reminds me about medications → I choose to take them.
- **Finances:** AI organizes bills → I decide which bills to pay first.

- Family: AI drafts letters → I add my personal stories.

This plan becomes your personal blueprint for independence.

Story: Gloria's Peace of Mind

Gloria lived alone and sometimes worried about what would happen if she became forgetful.

She asked AI: Create a weekly checklist for living alone, including safety reminders and errands.

The list included locking doors, checking smoke detectors, and reviewing her grocery stock. Gloria followed it faithfully.

"I don't feel vulnerable anymore," she said. "I feel prepared. That gives me peace of mind."

Closing Summary: Freedom With Support

Here's the lesson of this chapter:

- Independence doesn't mean refusing help. It means choosing tools that let you live life on your terms.
- AI can support independence in health, finances, safety, and mobility.
- Case studies show real people reclaiming confidence and dignity by using AI wisely.
- Reflection exercises help you identify where AI can free you while keeping you in charge.

Independence is not about clinging to the past. It's about embracing what helps you move forward with strength and dignity.

AI is not your replacement. It's your ally. It won't take away your freedom; it will help you protect it.

In the next chapter, we'll explore another vital part of thriving in the AI era: staying financially smart.

From budgeting to protecting against scams, you'll see how AI can be your partner in making wise money choices.

Chapter 10: Staying Financially Smart

Money and Peace of Mind

Why Money Matters More Than Ever

For many people, the later stages of life aren't about chasing wealth; they're about protecting what they have and making it last.

Money becomes less about status and more about security, freedom, and peace of mind.

Yet finances can feel more complicated than ever. Online banking, digital payments, new fees, confusing insurance policies, it's a lot to keep up with.

The good news? AI can be a guide. It can't make financial decisions for you, but it can help you understand, organize, and protect your money.

Story: Robert's Retirement Plan

Robert always managed his household finances with pen and paper. When retirement came, he felt lost.

Investments, Medicare, taxes, it was overwhelming.

He asked AI: Explain my retirement options in simple language.

Compare staying with my current plan versus moving to an annuity. Use bullet points.

The AI broke it down clearly. Robert still met with a financial advisor, but he walked in with sharper questions and more confidence.

"I didn't hand over my money decisions," he said. "I took back my clarity."

The Biggest Financial Fears

When people talk about money worries, they usually fall into four categories:

- **Running out of money**, will my savings last?

- **Making mistakes**, what if I misunderstand paperwork or terms?
- **Getting scammed**, what if I'm tricked?
- Losing independence, what if someone else takes over my finances?

AI can help with each of these, not by replacing financial professionals, but by acting as a translator, organizer, and protector.

Everyday Ways AI Supports Financial Smarts

- Budgeting

Prompt: Create a monthly budget for $3,000 income, including rent, groceries, transportation, and savings.

Result: A simple plan you can adjust, not a confusing spreadsheet.

- Bills and Deadlines

Prompt: Organize these six bills into a calendar with due dates and amounts.

Result: Peace of mind that nothing will slip through the cracks.

- Understanding Terms

Prompt: Explain "deductible" in plain English, with an example using car insurance.

Result: Clarity instead of confusion.

- Comparisons

Prompt: Compare the pros and cons of traditional Medicare versus Medicare Advantage, in plain language.

Result: Information that helps you ask better questions before deciding.

Reflection Exercise: Where Do I Feel Lost with Money?

Take out your notebook and answer honestly:

1. Do I struggle more with **budgeting**, **bills**, **financial terms**, or **long-term planning**?
2. Which one drains the most of my confidence?

Circle it. That's where AI can start helping you regain control.

Staying Financially Smart

AI as Your Money Organizer

Budgeting Without the Stress

Traditional budgeting tools can feel overwhelming: spreadsheets, categories, charts. Many people give up before they begin.

AI simplifies the process. Instead of setting up complicated software, you can just type a question in plain English.

Prompts to try:

- Create a budget for $2,500 monthly income. Include rent ($900), groceries, utilities, car payment, and leave room for savings.
- Suggest three ways to cut $100 from my monthly expenses without reducing food quality.

Instead of staring at numbers, you get a simple plan that feels manageable.

Story: Alice's Fresh Start. Alice always avoided budgeting. "It made me feel guilty," she admitted.

With AI, she asked for a budget that included money for small joys like coffee outings and craft supplies.

"It didn't feel like punishment anymore," she said. "It felt like freedom, because now I knew I could afford the things that matter to me."

Bills and Reminders

Missed bills lead to late fees and stress. AI can turn a pile of paperwork into a neat calendar.

Prompt: Organize these bills, electricity due the 12th, internet the 15th, insurance the 20th, and rent the 1st, into a monthly calendar.

Suggest reminders three days before each due date.

AI can also create tables that show bills by week, so you're never caught off guard.

Simplifying Financial Language

Banks, insurance companies, and investment firms often use jargon that feels like another language. AI can translate.

Prompts to try:

- Explain "deductible" like I'm 10 years old, with a car insurance example.
- Summarize the difference between APR and APY in plain English.
- What does "required minimum distribution" mean for retirement accounts? Give me an example.

When you understand the terms, you feel more confident making choices.

Comparing Options

Sometimes financial stress comes from too many choices. AI can help you compare.

Prompt: Compare the pros and cons of paying off my car loan early versus investing that money in savings.

Explain in plain English.

This doesn't replace a financial advisor. But it prepares you to walk into conversations informed and ready.

Story: Leon's Insurance

Leon was overwhelmed by health insurance options. "Every plan sounded the same," he said.

He asked AI: Compare three Medicare Advantage plans in plain English. Focus on premiums, copays, and coverage for prescriptions.

AI broke it into a simple chart. Leon still called a professional before choosing, but for the first time, he felt in control of the conversation.

Guided Exercise: My AI Money Helper

Take out your notebook.

Write down three areas of money that frustrate you. Examples:

- Budgeting
- Paying bills on time
- Understanding financial terms

For each, write one AI prompt you could try.

Example:

- Area: Budgeting

Prompt: Create a monthly budget for $3,000 income, including $1,200 rent, $400 groceries, $150 utilities, and at least $300 savings.

- Area: Bills

Prompt: Organize my monthly bills into a calendar with due dates and reminders.

- Area: Terms

Prompt: Explain the difference between fixed and variable interest rates, with examples.

Try one prompt this week. Notice how much lighter you feel when the fog clears.

Sidebar: AI as Your Translator

Think of AI as your translator between "financial language" and "real language."

Just as you'd use a dictionary for a foreign word, you can use AI for financial terms.

Clarity is power.

Staying Financially Smart

Protecting Against Scams

The Rise of Smarter Scams

AI isn't just in your hands; scammers use it too.

They can generate fake emails that look official, create voices that sound like loved ones, and write messages polished enough to fool anyone.

That makes vigilance more important than ever. But don't let this frighten you; let it prepare you.

Common Red Flags

- **Urgency:** "Act now or lose your account!"
- **Unfamiliar links:** Buttons that lead to strange websites.
- **Requests for personal info:** Banks or government agencies don't ask for Social Security numbers by email or text.
- Too good to be true: Promises of prizes, inheritances, or

investment "guarantees."

If something feels off, it probably is.

Story: Clara's "Bank" Email

Clara received an email warning her that her account was locked. The logo looked real, and the message was urgent.

She nearly clicked the link but stopped to ask AI: Does this email look like a scam?

The AI pointed out the misspellings and suspicious link. Clara deleted it, saving herself from fraud.

"That one pause," she said, "protected me."

How AI Helps Guard Your Wallet

You can use AI as a second set of eyes:

- *Check if this email looks suspicious.*
- *Summarize this investment opportunity in plain English. Does anything sound unrealistic?*
- Remind me of the safest steps for online shopping.

AI doesn't replace caution, but it reinforces it.

Exercise: My Scam Shield

Take your notebook. Write down three actions you'll take when faced with a suspicious message. For example:

1. Pause, don't click right away.
2. Verify, call the company directly.
3. Ask AI, have it check the language for red flags.

This becomes your personal scam shield.

Reflection: Financial Confidence

Financial stress often comes not just from lack of money, but from lack of clarity.

Ask yourself:

1. Do I understand where my money goes each month?
2. Do I feel in control of my bills?
3. Do I know how to spot a scam?

Circle the area where you feel weakest. Then, write one AI prompt you can try this week to strengthen it.

Example:

Weak area: bills → Prompt: Organize my bills into a monthly schedule with due dates.

Each step builds confidence.

Story: Henry's Calm

Henry used to dread the mailbox. "Every envelope felt like bad news," he admitted.

After using AI to create a budget, organize bills, and double-check suspicious emails, he felt different.

"I'm not afraid anymore," he said. "I know what to do."

That calm wasn't about having more money. It was about having more confidence.

Closing Summary: Clarity Is Power

Here's what this chapter taught us:

- Money matters because it provides freedom and peace of mind.
- AI can simplify budgeting, bills, and confusing terms.

- It can't replace financial advisors, but it can prepare you to make smarter decisions.
- Scams are getting smarter, but awareness and AI tools can protect you.
- Confidence comes not from having every answer, but from knowing where to turn for clarity.

Your finances are part of your independence. They're not just numbers; they're your freedom to live life on your terms.

AI is not here to control your money. It's here to help you understand it, organize it, and protect it, so you can focus on living.

In the next chapter, we'll shift from money to meaning, exploring how AI can help you find purpose and creativity in the AI era.

Part II: Actionable Prompts Resource Guide

Chapter Focus	Goal	Prompt Template (P.A.T.H. P-Step)
Ch 6: Learning	Start a new hobby/skill.	"Create a 7-day beginner's plan to learn in 15-minute lessons. Use metaphors to explain technical terms."
Ch 7: Time Savers	Organize daily chaos/time.	"Organize this to-do list into high-priority and low-priority tasks: [List]. Suggest a workflow automation strategy for home maintenance." [2]
Ch 8: Connection	Capture family memories.	"Turn this memory into a short, warm story. Add dialogue and keep the tone nostalgic."
Ch 9: Independence	Manage complex health info.	"Explain this medical report [Paste details] in plain English, focusing only on what three actions I need to take."
Ch 10: Finance	Create a simple budget.	"Act as a personal finance advisor. My monthly income is [Amount]. Help me create a simple monthly budget using the

		50/30/20 rule." [3]

Chapter 11: Finding Purpose and Creativity

Rediscovering Purpose

Why Purpose Matters

When people talk about happiness later in life, one word comes up more than any other: purpose.

Purpose isn't about a career or paycheck; it's about knowing your life still has meaning, direction, and impact.

Purpose might be found in relationships, hobbies, faith, volunteering, or creative projects. Without it, days can feel empty.

With it, even ordinary moments feel alive.

Story: Evelyn's Quilt

Evelyn retired from teaching and suddenly felt adrift. "I didn't know who I was without the classroom," she said.

One day, she asked AI: Suggest meaningful projects for someone who loves sewing and wants to bless others.

The AI suggested quilting for hospitals and shelters. Evelyn began making quilts for premature babies.

"It gave me a reason to get up every morning," she said. "And each quilt carried love forward."

AI didn't create her purpose, but it pointed her back to it.

How AI Sparks Purpose

AI can help you:

- **Discover opportunities:** *Suggest volunteer roles in my community that use my skills in teaching and mentoring.*
- **Rekindle old passions:** *Give me a 30-day plan to get back into painting*

after many years.

- Create structure: Help me set weekly goals for writing my memoir.

Sometimes we just need a nudge, a plan, or a reminder that purpose can be built from what we already love.

Reflection Exercise: Where Do I Feel Most Alive?

Take out your notebook. Write down three times in your life when you felt deeply fulfilled.

Ask yourself:

1. What was I doing?
2. Who was I serving or connecting with?
3. How could I bring a piece of that back into my life now?

Now, create a prompt for AI: Suggest three ways I can bring [that activity] into my current life, step by step.

Finding Purpose and Creativity

AI as Your Creativity Partner

Creativity Isn't Just for Artists

Many people shy away from the word "creative." They say, "I'm not an artist" or "I don't have a creative bone in my body."

But creativity isn't limited to painting or music. It's in the way you cook a meal, tell a story, solve a problem, or decorate a space.

Creativity is simply bringing something new into the world.

AI can't replace your imagination, but it can give it a boost, like a friend who tosses out ideas when you're stuck.

Writing with AI

Writing can feel intimidating, whether it's a poem, story, or family memoir. AI can act as a gentle co-writer.

Prompts to try:

- *Write a poem about autumn leaves in a warm, reflective tone.*
- *Help me draft the introduction to my family history book.*
- Create a bedtime story about a turtle who learns to dance.

The drafts AI creates aren't the final word; they're clay. You shape them with your details, emotions, and memories.

Story: Margaret's Memoir Margaret had boxes of journals, but didn't know how to turn them into a memoir.

She asked AI: Organize these journal entries into themes for a life story, such as childhood, career, family, and lessons learned.

AI gave her an outline. Margaret filled in her stories.

"It felt like having an editor who never judged me," she said.

Visual Art and Design

AI can also generate visual inspiration. While professional artists use advanced tools, everyday users can experiment with simple ones.

Prompts to try:

- *Create a painting-style image of a sunflower field at sunset.*
- *Design a greeting card with cheerful colors and flowers.*
- Suggest ten creative quilt patterns with color schemes.

The joy isn't in producing a masterpiece, it's in exploring.

Music and Sound

Some AI tools generate music or suggest chord progressions. You don't need to read sheet music to enjoy experimenting.

Prompts to try:

- *Compose a simple melody in a joyful mood, suitable for guitar.*
- Suggest lyrics for a song about family and home.

Even if you never perform, playing with sound can rekindle joy.

Storytelling and Legacy Projects

Perhaps the most meaningful use of AI creativity is in preserving your story.

Prompts to try:

- *Write a short story about the summer I met my best friend in 1965. Keep it nostalgic and warm.*
- *Turn these family recipes into a cookbook format with introductions.*
- *Help me draft a legacy letter for my grandchildren, sharing advice and love.*

Story: Thomas's Letters Thomas wanted to leave words of wisdom for his grandchildren, but didn't know how to begin.

He asked AI: Help me write ten short letters with life lessons, one about kindness, one about honesty, one about perseverance.

The AI drafted frameworks. Thomas rewrote them in his voice. His grandchildren now treasure those letters as keepsakes.

Guided Exercise: A Creative Spark

Take out your notebook. Pick one of these starting points:

- A story you want to capture
- A recipe you want to preserve
- A poem you want to write

- A design idea for a craft, quilt, or project

Write a simple AI prompt: Help me create [your idea].

Keep it simple and warm, and let me add personal touches.

Review what AI gives you. Circle what sparks joy. Cross out what doesn't fit. Add your own flair.

The goal isn't perfection. It's a play.

Sidebar: Why Creativity Heals

Research shows creative activity lowers stress, improves memory, and boosts mood.

It's not about the product; it's about the process.

AI lowers the barrier to entry, making creativity accessible for anyone, anytime.

Finding Purpose and Creativity

Purpose in Action

- **Case Study 1: Janet the Storyteller**

Janet always loved telling bedtime stories to her children and grandchildren, but felt her imagination had run dry.

She asked AI: Create a bedtime story about a brave squirrel who saves his forest friends.

The AI gave her a draft. Janet added her own twists, giving the characters names from her family.

Soon, her grandchildren were begging for "Grandma's new stories."

"I didn't think I had more stories left in me," Janet said. "Turns out, I just needed a little spark."

- **Case Study 2: Michael's Legacy Project**

Michael wanted to capture his family's immigration story but felt overwhelmed.

He asked AI: Help me draft a short history of my family moving from Italy to the U.S. in 1954. Organize it into sections: why they left, the journey, and starting a new life.

The AI produced a structure. Michael filled in memories, old letters, and family photos.

He printed a small book for his grandchildren.

"They finally understood the sacrifices," he said. "It gave them pride, and it gave me peace."

- **Case Study 3: Rosa's Community Cookbook**

Rosa was part of a church group that wanted to create a community cookbook but didn't know where to start.

She asked AI: Organize 40 recipes into categories, and suggest introductions that highlight faith, family, and friendship.

Within weeks, the group had a polished cookbook to sell as a fundraiser.

Rosa smiled: "AI didn't cook the meals or write the stories, we did. But it gave us a framework we couldn't have built alone."

Reflection: What Gives Me Meaning?

Purpose isn't found in grand achievements; it's found in small, meaningful acts.

AI can't tell you what matters most, but it can help you pursue it once you know.

Take out your notebook. Write answers to these questions:

1. What activities make me lose track of time because I enjoy them so much?

2. What skills or experiences do I want to pass on to others?

3. What's one small project I could start this month that would bring me joy?

Now, write an AI prompt for one of your answers. Example:

- *Help me design a memory book with photos and short captions for my grandchildren.*
- *Suggest three small volunteer projects I can do from home using my teaching background.*

Story: Harold's Song

Harold always dreamed of writing a song, but never tried.

He asked AI: Help me write lyrics for a song about gratitude, in a simple style I can sing with my guitar.

The AI gave him a draft. Harold tweaked it until it reflected his heart.

When he sang it at a family gathering, his children wept.

"It wasn't perfect," Harold said, "but it was me. That's what mattered."

Closing Summary: Purpose + Creativity = Legacy

Here's what this chapter taught us:

- Purpose gives life meaning at any stage.
- Creativity isn't about talent, it's about expression.
- AI can act as a spark, offering drafts, ideas, and frameworks.
- Real people are already using AI to tell stories, preserve memories, and create art.

Your purpose isn't something AI invents. It's something you

rediscover with its help.

At its heart, AI is a tool. What you create with it, stories, songs, quilts, cookbooks, letters, becomes your legacy.

Purpose is what wakes you up in the morning. Creativity is what gives color to your days.

Together, they remind you that no matter your age, your story is still being written.

And with AI as your companion, you'll have fresh tools to tell it beautifully.

In the next chapter, we'll explore the flip side of creativity: navigating change and uncertainty.

Because thriving in the AI era isn't just about joy, it's about resilience when things shift quickly.

Chapter 12: Navigating Change and Uncertainty

Facing the Unknown

Why Change Feels Harder Now

Change has always been part of life: new jobs, new towns, new family roles.

But today's changes, especially in technology, feel different.

They come faster, they touch every part of daily life, and they seem harder to control.

For many people, the thought of keeping up feels overwhelming.

"I just got used to smartphones," someone might say, "and now I'm supposed to understand artificial intelligence?"

The truth is: you don't need to master everything. You just need to learn how to live well with change.

Story: Doris and the ATM

When ATMs first appeared in the 1970s, Doris refused to use them.

"I don't trust a machine with my money," she said. For years, she stood in line at the bank instead.

One day, pressed for time, she tried an ATM. It worked perfectly.

"I realized the machine wasn't my enemy," Doris later admitted. "It was my shortcut."

The ATM didn't end her independence; it extended it.

The same will be true for AI.

The Three Truths About Change

1. **Change is constant.** Technology, culture, and habits will always shift. Fighting it only exhausts you.

2. **Change feels personal.** It challenges routines, traditions, and even identity. That's why it stirs emotions.

3. **Change creates opportunity.** Each new shift opens doors, if you're willing to walk through them.

Reflection Exercise: My Change Story

Think back on one big change you've already survived:

- Moving to a new home
- Adapting to email or cell phones
- Transitioning into retirement

Write down:

1. What scared me most at the time?
2. How did I adapt?
3. What strengths did I discover?

This exercise reminds you: you've navigated change before. You can do it again.

Navigating Change and Uncertainty

Building Confidence in Uncertainty

Why Uncertainty Feels Scary

Uncertainty triggers anxiety because the brain craves predictability. When you don't know what's coming, you imagine the worst.

But uncertainty is also where growth happens. Every major turning point, from starting a family to retiring, began with uncertainty.

AI is simply the latest version of that.

- **Strategy 1: Focus on What You Can Control**

You can't control how fast AI evolves. You can control:

- Whether you try it in small ways.
- What information do you trust?
- How you spend your energy and time.

When you shrink your focus to what's within reach, fear loses its grip.

Story: Gerald's First Prompt

Gerald resisted AI until his granddaughter said, "Grandpa, just ask it one question."

He typed: What are three easy soup recipes with chicken and vegetables?

When he saw the simple, clear answer, he laughed. "That wasn't scary at all."

Control returned the moment he took one small step.

- **Strategy 2: Break Change into Small Steps**

Instead of thinking, "I have to learn AI," reframe it as:

- Try one prompt this week.
- Use it for one daily task.
- Reflect on how it helped.

Small steps build momentum.

- **Strategy 3: Use AI as a Safety Net**

Uncertainty often comes from fear of mistakes. But AI can serve as a second set of eyes.

- Draft an email → Ask AI to review for clarity.
- Organize bills → Ask AI to double-check deadlines.

- Learn a new recipe → Ask AI for troubleshooting if it goes wrong.

  Instead of fearing mistakes, you gain confidence knowing you have backup.

- **Strategy 4: Build a Support System**

Facing change alone feels heavy. Facing it with others feels lighter. Share prompts, stories, and discoveries with friends or family.

One couple made a game of it: each week, they tried AI for a new household task.

They compared notes, laughed at funny outputs, and celebrated wins. Change became bonding instead of a burden.

Guided Exercise: My Change Toolkit

Take out your notebook. Write three columns:

What I Can't Control	**What I Can Control**	**My First Step This Week**
How AI evolves	My willingness to try small tasks	Write one AI prompt I will try before Sunday.
What companies invent	How I protect my privacy	
How society uses it	Where can I get trustworthy information?	
This reframes uncertainty as manageable. You may not control the storm, but you can control how you steer your boat.		

Story: Linda's Calm

Linda once panicked over every tech update. Now, she tries one small thing at a time.

"I don't need to master everything," she said. "I just need to learn enough to keep living life my way."

That calm didn't come from avoiding change; it came from pacing herself.

Navigating Change and Uncertainty

Resilience in Action

- **Case Study 1: Norman and the Smartphone**

  Norman resisted getting a smartphone for years. "I don't need all those apps," he insisted.

  Finally, when his flip phone stopped working, he gave in.

  At first, it felt foreign. But he asked AI: Explain five things I can do with my smartphone that will make my life easier.

  The list included taking photos, using maps, sending texts, setting alarms, and finding recipes.

  Within weeks, Norman was texting his grandchildren daily. "I was afraid of the change," he said.

  "Now I can't imagine life without it."

- **Case Study 2: Helen and Online Banking**

  Helen didn't trust online banking. But as branches closed, she felt she had no choice.

  She asked AI: Explain online banking in plain language. What steps keep it safe?

  AI broke it into clear, simple actions: use strong passwords, log out after sessions, never click on suspicious links.

Helen tried it first to check balances, then to pay a bill.

"It saved me two hours in line," she said. "I felt like I'd reclaimed my time, not lost control."

- **Case Study 3: Marcus the Mentor**

Marcus worked in manufacturing before retirement. When AI started making headlines, he feared it would erase the jobs he once held.

But instead of retreating, he asked AI: Explain how AI is being used in factories today.

He discovered that while some jobs changed, new roles opened too, in maintenance, oversight, and design.

Marcus began mentoring younger workers, helping them navigate transitions with wisdom.

"I can't stop change," he said, "but I can help others walk through it."

Reflection: Adapting with Grace

Adapting to change doesn't mean pretending it's easy. It means approaching it with curiosity instead of fear, with patience instead of panic. Ask yourself:

1. What changes once scared me, but I now take for granted?
2. How did I get through those transitions?
3. What would it look like to face AI with the same grace?

Write a short reflection in your notebook. Title it: "I've Done This Before."

Because you have.

Story: Anna's Garden

Anna once resisted new gardening methods. She preferred "the way we've always done it." But when she tried a new irrigation system her son suggested, her garden flourished. Reflecting, she said: "At first, I felt like change was stealing my tradition. Then I realized it was giving me more of what I love."

AI, like the irrigation system, isn't about replacing what you love. It's about helping it grow.

Closing Summary: The Art of Resilience

Here's what this chapter taught us:

- Change is constant, but you've navigated it before.
- Uncertainty feels scary, but small steps restore control.
- AI can serve as a safety net and guide, not a threat.
- Real people, like Norman, Helen, Marcus, and Anna, are already adapting with grace.

Resilience isn't about never feeling fear. It's about moving forward anyway.

The world will keep changing. AI will keep evolving. But your ability to adapt, learn, and choose your response is timeless.

You don't need to outrun change. You just need to walk through it steadily, with curiosity and courage.

In the next chapter, we'll go deeper into the future, asking not just how to survive today, but how to prepare for tomorrow.

What's next in the AI era, and how can you be ready for it?

Chapter 13: Preparing for Tomorrow

Why Preparation Matters

The Feeling of Falling Behind

Many people worry about being "left behind" as technology evolves. The pace can feel impossible to match. But preparation isn't about mastering every gadget or app; it's about creating habits that help you adapt smoothly. Preparation is less about predicting the future and more about being ready to adjust when it comes.

Story: Ellen and the Email Era

Ellen remembered when her workplace introduced email. She panicked. "I thought, how will I ever learn this?" At first, she wrote emails like formal letters. But gradually, she realized email was just another way to communicate.

Today, she uses it daily to keep up with her grandchildren.

The lesson? With preparation and patience, even big changes become part of everyday life.

The Three Pillars of Preparing for Tomorrow

- **Mindset:** Curiosity over fear. Ask "How could this help me?" instead of "What if this replaces me?"
- **Skillset:** Learning small, practical ways to use AI regularly. Practice makes it familiar.
- **Toolset:** Having simple systems, a notebook for prompts, a safe way to store passwords, and a routine for learning.

With these three pillars, tomorrow feels less threatening and more like an adventure.

Reflection Exercise: My Preparation Strengths

Write in your notebook:

1. Am I stronger in mindset, skillset, or toolset?
2. Which one do I need to build more of?
3. What's one step I could take this week to strengthen it?

Practical Preparation Habits

- Habit 1: Ongoing Learning

Make learning a routine, not a one-time event. Even 15 minutes a week experimenting with AI builds confidence.

Prompt to try: Show me one new way I can use AI this week to make life easier.

- **Habit 2: Safe Foundations**

Preparation means security. Protecting your information ensures you can explore AI without worry.

  - Use strong passwords.
  - Turn on two-factor authentication.
  - Be cautious with personal details.

Story: Paul's Passwords Paul kept his passwords written on scraps of paper.

After nearly losing access to his bank account, he used AI to help him set up a password manager.

> "It was like locking the doors to my house for the first time," he said.

- **Habit 3: Practice with Purpose**

Don't just use AI randomly. Choose meaningful goals.

- Write one family story per month.
- Plan meals weekly with AI.
- Use AI for one financial task, like organizing bills.

- **Habit 4: Build a community**

Preparing for tomorrow is easier when you're not alone. Share prompts, stories, and discoveries with friends or family.

Reflection Prompt: Who in my life could I share one AI skill with this month?

Guided Exercise: My "Future-Ready Routine"

Take your notebook. Write down three actions you'll repeat each week:

1. Learn one new thing with AI.
2. Use AI for one practical task (meal planning, writing, organizing).
3. Share one discovery with a friend or family member.

This routine keeps you prepared without overwhelm.

Confidence for Tomorrow

- **Case Study 1: Clara the Curious**

Clara made a habit of trying one new AI feature each week.

Over a year, she grew from anxious to confident. "I'm not ahead of the kids," she laughed, "but I'm not behind either."

- **Case Study 2: Daniel the Planner**

Daniel wanted to ensure his finances and healthcare were future-proof.

He asked AI: List five things I should organize now to make the next decade easier for my family and me.

The AI suggested updating wills, organizing medical records, planning budgets, and backing up family photos.

Daniel tackled them one by one. "I feel ready," he said.

- **Case Study 3: Ruth the Legacy Builder**

Ruth used AI to prepare her family history, recipes, and letters for her grandchildren.

"The future isn't about me keeping up with machines," she said. "It's about leaving something lasting for my family."

Reflection: What Future Am I Preparing For?

Ask yourself:

1. Do I want more **freedom**?
2. Do I want more **security**?
3. Do I want to leave more legacy?

Circle the one that matters most. Then write one AI prompt you could try this week to prepare in that area.

Closing Summary: Tomorrow Is Built Today

Here's the lesson of this chapter:

- Preparation is less about predicting tomorrow and more about steady habits today.
- Mindset, skillset, and toolset form the foundation of readiness.
- Habits like learning weekly, protecting information, and sharing knowledge build resilience.
- Real people are already preparing through small, steady steps.

The future doesn't belong only to the young or the technical.

It belongs to the curious, the willing, and the prepared.

Tomorrow is uncertain, but with the right habits, you can meet it with confidence.

Chapter 14: The Future of AI and You

Looking Ahead Without Fear

The Speed of Tomorrow

Technology moves faster than ever. AI today can write essays, generate art, and help with planning.

Tomorrow, it may handle medical research, design buildings, or discover new treatments.

For many, that pace feels dizzying. But here's the truth: you don't need to know it all.

You only need to know enough to keep your footing, to stay safe, and to use what benefits you.

The future of AI isn't about replacing people; it's about reshaping how we live and work.

Story: Sam's Perspective

Sam remembered when computers first came to his workplace. "Everyone panicked," he said. "We thought they'd take our jobs."

Instead, the computers made tasks easier. "It wasn't the end of work," Sam reflected.

"It was the start of new kinds of work."

AI will feel the same. It will close some doors and open others, and the real key is to be open to walking through.

The Four Likely Directions of AI's Future

1. **Healthcare Partner**, AI will increasingly help doctors detect illness earlier, track health, and provide personalized care plans.

2. **Workforce Helper**, AI will reshape jobs, but also create new roles in oversight, design, and creativity.
3. **Personal Copilot**, Everyday tasks will become even more streamlined, from home maintenance to travel planning.
4. **Creative Collaborator**, AI will continue to spark art, music, and stories, but the heart will remain human.

Reflection: My Hopes for the Future

Take your notebook. Write down:

1. One way I hope AI makes life easier.
2. One way I hope AI makes life more joyful.
3. One thing I want to keep fully human.

This reflection sets the tone: the future is not just about what AI does, but about what you choose to preserve.

The Human Role in an AI World

What Will Never Change

Even as AI grows smarter, certain human qualities will always matter:

- **Compassion**, Machines can mimic empathy, but only people can truly care.
- **Wisdom**, Experience, and perspective come only from living.
- **Connection**, AI can draft words, but only you can love.
- **Creativity,** AI can generate, but only people can bring soul.

The future of AI isn't about surrendering these things. It's about using AI to clear away clutter so we can focus on them more deeply.

Story: Grace and the Grandchildren

Grace used AI to draft letters to her grandchildren, but she always added her own stories and humor.

Her granddaughter later said, "Grandma, the letters sound like you. AI just helped you send more of them."

That's the key: AI amplifies humanity, it doesn't erase it.

The Role of Lifelong Learning

The people who thrive in the AI era will not be the youngest or the most technical.

They'll be the ones most willing to keep learning.

Lifelong learning means curiosity stays alive. It means saying, "Show me," instead of, "It's too late for me."

Prompt to try: Suggest three small ways to keep learning about AI each month without being overwhelmed.

Guided Exercise: My Human Priorities

Write three statements in your notebook:

1. In the AI era, I will protect my ability to…
2. I will use AI to give me more time for…
3. I will teach my children or grandchildren that…

These lock in your vision of what matters most.

Walking Into the Future with Confidence

- **Case Study 1: Leo the Explorer**

Leo once resisted every new technology. But after trying AI for meal planning, then for writing family history, he realized: "The future isn't about machines taking over. It's about me choosing how to use them."

He now teaches other retirees how to use AI in small ways. His motto: "The future belongs to the curious."

- **Case Study 2: Martha's Legacy**

Martha worried about leaving a legacy for her grandchildren. With AI's help, she wrote stories of her childhood, organized photos, and even recorded voice notes.

On her 80th birthday, her family presented her with a book they had compiled from her AI-assisted projects.

"You gave us your story," her daughter said. "That's more valuable than anything else."

Reflection: Writing Your Next Chapter

You've now walked through the fears, the opportunities, the practical tools, and the possibilities of AI.

Ask yourself:

1. What small step will I take this week to use AI in a way that supports my life?
2. What role do I want AI to play in the story of my future?
3. What story do I want my loved ones to remember about how I faced change?

These reflections turn knowledge into action, and action into legacy.

Closing Summary: The Future Is a Partnership

Here's the truth: AI will keep evolving. The pace may feel dizzying at times. But the future is not about AI replacing humanity; it's about humans and AI working together.

AI can organize, translate, and generate.

You can love, choose, and create meaning.

Together, that makes for a future where life feels lighter, richer, and more connected.

The AI era isn't something to survive. It's something to live, fully, bravely, and joyfully.

Your story is still being written. And with curiosity and courage, you'll write the next chapter beautifully.

Epilogue: Your Next Chapter

Section 1: Looking Back at the Journey

When you first opened this book, you may have felt anxious, skeptical, or even fearful about AI. You weren't alone.

Millions of people share those same worries.

But as you've read, you've seen that AI is not a shadow creeping in to replace you.

It's a tool, sometimes a powerful one, sometimes a simple one, that can lighten your load, spark your creativity, and give you more time for the things that truly matter.

Think back through the chapters:

- In **Chapter 1**, you learned that fear of AI is natural, but fear fades with understanding.
- In **Chapter 4**, you saw AI as your copilot, there to assist but never to control.
- In **Chapter 7**, you discovered how everyday tasks can be made simpler, giving you back time.
- In **Chapter 9**, you found ways AI can protect your independence, allowing you to live life on your terms.
- In **Chapter 11**, you rediscovered purpose and creativity, with AI sparking your imagination rather than replacing it.
- **In Chapters 13 and 14**, you looked toward tomorrow, learning that preparation, not perfection, is the real key.

This journey has not been about mastering technology. It has been about mastering perspective.

You don't need to know everything about AI. You just need to know enough to make it work for you.

Section 2: The Heart of It All, Human First

Through all the examples and exercises, one truth has stayed steady: AI is a tool, not a replacement for what makes you human.

- **Love** cannot be automated.
- **Wisdom** cannot be programmed.
- **Connection** cannot be downloaded.
- **Legacy** cannot be faked.

These are yours to give. AI may help you write the letter, capture the story, or plan the event, but only you bring the heart, the humor, the tenderness, the lived experience.

If you take only one message from this book, let it be this: AI can do many things, but it cannot replace you.

Section 3: Writing Your Next Chapter

Every reader closes a book at a different place in life. Some may be just beginning to experiment with AI.

Others may already be curious explorers. Wherever you stand, the next chapter is yours to write.

Here are three simple commitments you can carry forward:

1. Stay Curious

   Ask one new question of AI each week. Small steps build comfort.

2. Stay Grounded

   Protect your data, question scams, and trust your judgment.

3. Stay Human

Use AI to save time and energy so you can invest in relationships, creativity, and meaning.

Think of these as your compass points. No matter how quickly technology shifts, these guideposts will keep you steady.

Reflection Exercise: My Promise to Myself

Take out your notebook one final time. Write this heading: "My Promise for the AI Era."

Complete the sentence:

1. I will use AI to…
2. I will protect my independence by…
3. I will leave a legacy of…

This is your declaration. Your anchor. Your roadmap.

Section 4: A Closing Word of Encouragement

The AI era will bring surprises, some wonderful, some challenging. But then again, so has every era.

You've already weathered changes that once felt impossible: from rotary phones to smartphones, from typewriters to computers, from letters to video calls.

Each time, you adapted. Each time, you grew. And each time, you discovered that technology didn't erase your humanity, it gave you new ways to express it.

AI is simply the next chapter in that same story.

So, step forward not with fear, but with curiosity. Step forward not with hesitation, but with confidence.

Step forward knowing that you have the tools, the wisdom, and the courage to not just survive in the AI era, but to thrive.

The world still needs your voice. Your creativity. Your guidance. Your love.

The story of the AI era is still being written. And the most important part of it is you.

One-Page Key Takeaways: Your AI Confidence Checklist

Category	**Action Item**	**Chapter Reference**
Mindset	Recognize that fear is natural, but choose curiosity over avoidance.	Ch. 1, 2
Strategy	Use AI as a Copilot to replace *tasks*, reserving time for human judgment and connection.	Ch. 3, 4
Safety	Enable Two-Factor Authentication (2FA) and use the Deepfake Checklist before reacting to urgent requests.	Ch. 5
Daily Use	Leverage the P.A.T.H. Method (Prompt, Context, Try Again, Handoff) for all AI interactions.	Ch. 4
Time & Focus	Allow AI to handle repetitive tasks (scheduling, drafting) to reclaim time for joy and legacy.	Ch. 7, 8

Independence	Use AI as a tool to simplify financial terms and medical instructions, maintaining clarity and control.	Ch. 9, 10
Legacy	Use AI to structure memories and wisdom into stories, recipes, or letters for future generations.	Ch. 11[4]
Resilience	Understand that mastering everything is unnecessary; small, steady learning steps build confidence for tomorrow.	Ch. 12, 13

Works cited

1. How to Protect Yourself Against Deepfakes - National Cybersecurity Alliance, accessed November 1, 2025, https://www.staysafeonline.org/articles/how-to-protect-yourself-against-deepfakes

2. McKinsey & Company. A Future That Works: Automation, Employment, and Productivity. https://www.mckinsey.com

3. Warren, Elizabeth, and Amelia Warren Tyagi. *All Your Worth: The Ultimate Lifetime Money Plan.* Free Press, 2005.

4. Gulotta, Rebecca, et al. "Digital Preservation of Personal Memories." MIT Media Lab, Massachusetts Institute of Technology.

Made in the USA
Monee, IL
04 November 2026

67382311R00079